"William Webb is becoming one of evangelicalism's finest teachers of how to 'live the Bible' in our world. What he teaches us is simple: each text in the Bible is embedded in a historical context, and the only way to read the Bible responsibly is to see what the Bible was saying in that historical context. When it comes to living out the Bible in our world, we watch how God teaches his people to redeem those historical contexts. This book applies that method to corporal punishment with stunningly redemptive conclusions. Every parent and every pastor, in that order, needs to read this book before either lifts a hand or teaches others to lift a hand. I pray this book will flourish."

Scot McKnight, professor in religious studies, North Park University

"How do we apply to our lives biblical texts written to ancient audiences in radically different social and cultural contexts than our own? That is the real question Professor Webb wrestles with in this engaging and thoughtful book. This volume presents a compelling case that contemporary pro-spankers are not adopting a more 'biblical' approach to discipline, but are rather going beyond the Bible to recontextualizing biblical texts on the basis of contemporary pediatric, social and psychological concerns. In other words, they are (without realizing it) adopting a redemptive-movement hermeneutic not so different from the one Webb advocates. This book should be read by every Christian interested in child raising and discipline. More importantly, it should be read by every Christian interested in how to read and apply God's Word in our rapidly changing world."

Mark L. Strauss, professor of New Testament, Bethel Seminary–San Diego

"To spank or not to spank is not a question from Shakespeare but one most parents ask. Thinking through what it means to parent well biblically is a key Christian concern. This book takes you through the paces well autobiographically and will cause you to think about what you do and why. It will also cause you to reflect on how the Bible teaches us. Both are great lessons for parents and believers."

Darrell Bock, Research Professor of New Testament, Dallas Theological Seminary

"Webb wrestles gallantly with two difficult issues: (a) How should Christians read biblical texts that seem to advocate violent responses to situations calling for discipline? and (b) How should Christian parents handle difficult disciplinary situations involving their children? The author handles the biblical evidence carefully and exhibits great grace toward those who read and apply the evidence differently. Applying his 'redemptive-movement' hermeneutic persuasively to a specific ethical issue, he challenges readers to consider alternatives to corporal punishment in the home. This is a must-read for parents with young children, and for theologians who seek to apply the theology of texts from another time and another world to the contemporary context."

Daniel Block, professor of Old Testament, Wheaton College Graduate School

"When I read *Slaves, Women and Homosexuals,* I remember thinking, *I wish I could have written a book like this.* Now I had the same sense reading *Corporal Punishment in the Bible.* This book is about exercising parental discipline biblically by, paradoxically, disobeying the concrete-specific instructions in the Bible (in seven ways!) that speak to this subject. Contemporary pro-spankers have, indeed, already done this but do not adequately justify

how they could abandon an 'on the page' grammatical-historical exegesis of the corporal punishment texts to get there. In collaboration with Marilyn, his eminently qualified wife and mother of their three children, Bill includes chapters on the *why* and *how* of alternative discipline methods that I wish I could have applied when our children were in their pre-teens. I loved reading this book not only for the details of the topic he addresses but for the countless parallels, paradigms and ponderings that popped into my head as I considered the implications of being led by the Spirit for so many other aspects of biblical teaching."
William Heth, professor of biblical studies, Taylor University

"Webb challenges the premises of the traditional spanking position at a hermeneutical level and exposes its failure to come to grips with what the Bible actually says on the subject. He shows how most advocates of spanking have actually softened the Bible's teaching on the subject, and he commends them for doing so. Yet he mounts a convincing case for following that trajectory and going one step further, building his position on a redemptive-movement hermeneutic that most Christians already use when arguing for an antislavery viewpoint. Webb's logic is tight and his insights penetrating. But beyond this, perhaps what is most impressive is the humble, irenic spirit he displays as he explains how he arrived at his position and addresses those who disagree with him. It will be interesting to see how the pro-spanking position responds to this thoughtful and profound challenge. This reviewer suspects that many will find Webb's book a breath of fresh air."
Robert Chisholm, professor of Old Testament, Dallas Theological Seminary

"The implications of this book go far beyond disturbing ancient requirements of physical punishment and present-day challenges of child discipline. I wish everyone who is interested in doing grammatical-historical interpretation and application of the Scriptures could read the meticulous way William Webb works to find and unfold the Bible's own ultimate ethic. As many of us look for wisdom in moving forward, the author finds important conservative precedent in some surprising, yet already widely accepted, places."
Mart De Haan, president of RBC Ministries

"What does it mean to be 'biblical'? Bill Webb exposes just how easy it is for people to claim this without paying close attention to what the Bible actually says. He provides a case study in the redemptive-movement method of discerning and applying the ethical challenge of Old Testament texts. Since the corporal punishments of the Old Testament are among its more morally disturbing features, his reflection on this issue is both thorough and courageous. If none of us, one hopes, is doing or advocating 'what the Bible actually says' in exercising parental discipline, then how can we reach a principled theory and practice in that area that can still be defended as 'biblical' with interpretive integrity? This is a book that is both theologically challenging and yet realistically earthed in the mundane and moving experience of the Webb family. It describes a personal hermeneutical journey shared with fellow parents, as well as a hermeneutical conclusion offered to the academy. At both levels it deserves careful listening and response."
Christopher J. H. Wright, Langham Partnership International, author of *Old Testament Ethics for the People of God*

CORPORAL
PUNISHMENT
IN THE BIBLE

A Redemptive-Movement
Hermeneutic for Troubling Texts

WILLIAM J. WEBB

IVP Academic
An imprint of InterVarsity Press
Downers Grove, Illinois

InterVarsity Press
P.O. Box 1400, Downers Grove, IL 60515-1426
World Wide Web: www.ivpress.com
E-mail: email@ivpress.com

InterVarsity Press® is the book-publishing division of InterVarsity Christian Fellowship/USA®, a movement of
students and faculty active on campus at hundreds of universities, colleges and schools of nursing in the United States
of America, and a member movement of the International Fellowship of Evangelical Students. For information
about local and regional activities, write Public Relations Dept., InterVarsity Christian Fellowship/USA, 6400
Schroeder Rd., P.O. Box 7895, Madison, WI 53707-7895, or visit the IVCF website at <www.intervarsity.org>.

Scripture quotations, unless otherwise noted, are from the New Revised Standard Version of the Bible, *copyright*
1989 by the Division of Christian Education of the National Council of the Churches of Christ in the USA. Used by
permission. All rights reserved.

While all stories in this book are true, some names and identifying information have been changed to protect the
privacy of the individuals involved.

Cover design: Cindy Kiple
Interior design: Beth Hagenberg
Images: Dave Rau/iStockphoto

ISBN 978-0-8308-2761-9

Printed in the United States of America ∞

 InterVarsity Press is committed to protecting the environment and to the responsible use of natural
resources. As a member of Green Press Initiative we use recycled paper whenever possible. To learn
more about the Green Press Initiative, visit <www.greenpressinitiative.org>.

Library of Congress Cataloging-in-Publication Data

Webb, William J., 1957-
  Corporal punishment in the Bible: a redemptive-movement hermeneutic
for troubling texts/William J. Webb.
    p. cm.
  Includes bibliographical references and index.
  ISBN 978-0-8308-2761-9 (pbk.: alk. paper)
  1. Corporal punishment—Biblical teaching. 2. Corporal
punishment—Religious aspects—Christianity. 3. Bible—Hermeneutics.
I. Title.
  BS680.P78W43 2011
  220.8'36467—dc22

2011013665

P	19	18	17	16	15	14	13	12	11	10	9	8	7	6	5	4	3	2	1
Y	27	26	25	24	23	22	21	20	19	18	17	16	15	14	13	12	11			

To Marilyn,

My friend and companion in a twenty-four-year

adventure of raising children. You have taken this book

on hermeneutics and lived out its concepts with far more

grace and beauty than the world of academic theory.

TABLE OF CONTENTS

FOREWORD

Fairly early on in my school experience we had a teacher named Mr. Macdonald (known behind his back as "Dornieboy"), who was notorious for his use of the tawse (Scots for the "belt") administered on the palm of the hand for every misdemeanor, including in particular the scoring of a lower grade than his arbitrarily chosen pass mark in every class exercise and assignment. I never thought that it was wrong to punish pupils for disobedience and bad behavior, but I could not see how it was just for pupils to be punished for not reaching grades that were inherently beyond their capabilities. Fortunately I never fell into his clutches, but I was absolutely scared stiff lest I ever should do so (I was a coward regarding suffering and enduring pain), and he figured in my nightmares from time to time. Other people's recollections of early education in Scotland indicate that my Dumfries experience of inhumane teachers was far from exceptional.

Today the situation in Scotland is radically different, and a teacher can be dismissed for anything that remotely resembles physical action against unruly pupils even if they are acting violently and need to be restrained, and we may well wonder whether the sanctions against such behavior are realistic and adequate.

But what about the situation in the home, where parents may also be in danger of prosecution if they physically chastise their children? Particularly in North America there are Christians who affirm strongly the duty of parents to use physical chastisement on the basis of Scripture. Are those who differ from them to be regarded as disobeying biblical teaching and succumbing to secular liberalism?

This is the issue taken up in this book by Bill Webb, who makes a number of points. First, he demonstrates that those who claim to be following Scripture by advocating and practicing corporal punishment within the family in fact go "beyond Scripture" by making a number of corrections of Scriptural practice that make such chastisement significantly different with respect to its severity and general character. He applauds this shift. Second, he argues that in fact Scripture shows a redemptive trajectory when compared with the practices of other ancient people, and that all of those who reduce the severity of corporal punishment are taking further that trajectory which began in Scripture and has not yet reached its zenith. Third, he argues for the nonuse of corporal punishment and describes in helpful detail other strategies that have been tried and tested in his wife's and his own experience with their own family (including the care of a son with severe learning difficulties), so that the same scriptural aim of teaching children to practice good behavior is attainable by other sanctions that are free from the criticisms that can rightly be made of corporal punishment.

The argument is thus a specific example of the kind of biblical hermeneutics advocated in the author's earlier writings, especially his *Slaves, Women and Homosexuals* but also as summarized in his contribution to *Four Views on Moving Beyond the Bible to Theology*, edited by Gary Meadors. But where these other works tend to be more academic in their approach, this book has added a nonacademic postscript written at a more down-to-earth level, with an abundance of personal insight and experience as well as practical application that parents will find helpful. (I could have profited much from it if it had been published when Joyce and I were bringing up our four children.) Moreover, the approach is conciliatory and gracious toward those who are gently but firmly corrected for not realizing that their approach to Scripture does in fact lead them to move beyond what Scripture says while holding to the supreme authority of Scripture. Thus the book offers a compelling example of the basic rightness of Bill's approach to the problem of applying Scripture to such issues as "slavery, women and homosexuals," and so it will help to commend this hermeneutical key to those who may have been suspicious of it in the past. And that in its turn will forward what matters most to the author: the development and practice of behavior that is truly biblical and Christian, and so pleasing and glorifying to God as well as commending the gospel to the people.

In short, I enjoyed the book and could not put it down once I started to read it.

I. Howard Marshall

ACKNOWLEDGMENTS

This book has come into being through the contributions of many people. I must thank the staff at InterVarsity Press for their unfailing patience in working with probably the most delinquent author they have ever signed on. When we got the diagnosis of leukodystrophy with Jon (our oldest son), it meant a lot of changes for our family. Andy Le Peau and Gary Deddo met with me several times, once in San Diego with both Marilyn and myself. They prayed with us and assured us that they wanted to see a couple of "overdue books" come to completion. To my surprise they were not interested in closing out the overdue contracts. As of last summer Jon is now in a full-time care home just north of Waterloo, Ontario, and our lives are beginning to return to normal. I must express special thanks to Gary for helping me articulate the intersecting relationship between ethics and hermeneutics in an explicit fashion—some things remain dormant in one's mind until a perceptive editor offers some prodding questions. So thanks from myself and Marilyn to the entire IVP staff for your encouragement and blessing in our lives.

Many academic colleagues and friends have read over some or all of the chapters in this book. I thank my colleagues at Heritage College and Seminary for an unforgettable twenty-two-year pilgrimage together—their support and delightful exchange have made those years a cherished memory. I want to especially thank those who read and offered feedback on this book during its formation—Gord Oeste, Kelvin Mutter, Stan Fowler, David Smith, Cyril Guerette, David Barker, Paul Wilson, Cheryl Belch and Jim Cianca. I was also fortunate to receive input from several persons in pastoral ministry—in particular I wish to thank Rod Casey for his sustained encouragement and perceptive interaction. Mart DeHaan was kind enough to read the manuscript several times during its early stages and assist me in some crucial communication issues. Two gifted editors—Dorian Coover-Cox and Robert L. Webb—gave countless hours helping me write clearly and choose apt words. Their generous labors and friendship have been an inspiration and have produced a much better manuscript. In the final hours of finishing this project, when I was swamped with some other pressing matters, my youngest son, Joel (now a first-year university student!), gladly pitched in and developed the author index—a more wonderful gift I could not have had.

Finally, there is a group of close friends known as our "gourm club"—made up of Christians from various walks of life (*gourm* is short for gourmet). This eclectic group of five couples includes a teacher, a principal, a teaching assistant, four professors, a financial adviser, an administrative assistant, and a family and marriage counselor. We meet a half dozen times throughout the year and cook some fabulous dinners over four or five hours of conversation. The contents of these chapters were often bantered around among these long-time friends in both a playful and serious manner, depending on the moment. These friends stood with me through this past year, which has been a challenging period of transition.

At the end of this year I find myself as an adjunct professor at Tyndale Seminary in Toronto, Ontario. This acclaimed seminary within Canada has been gracious in offering me an academic home. I wish to thank the faculty of Tyndale Seminary and in particular the dean, Janet Clark, for your kind welcome and for giving me a place to hang my hat. I am indeed grateful to them.

ABBREVIATIONS

ANE	Ancient Near East(ern)
AOTC	Abingdon Old Testament Commentaries
BCOTWP	Baker Commentary on the Old Testament Wisdom and Psalms
HL	Hittite Laws
ITC	International Theological Commentary
LH	Laws of Hammurabi
MAL	Middle Assyrian Laws
MAPD	Middle Assyrian Palace Decrees
MH Letters	Middle Hittite Letters
NAC	New American Commentary
NIBC	New International Biblical Commentary
NICOT	New International Commentary on the Old Testament
NIVAC	New International Version Application Commentary
OBT	Overtures to Biblical Theology
OTS	Old Testament Studies
SBL	Studies in Biblical Literature
SHBC	Smith & Helwys Bible Commentary
VTSup	Supplements to Vetus Testamentum

INTRODUCTION

A TROUBLED CHRISTIAN SOUL

Within the Bible we encounter three very stark instruments of corporal punishment: the rod, the whip and the heavy knife. By far the rod and whip are mentioned most frequently. In one particular case, however, Scripture infers the use of a heavy knife or perhaps an ax for the cutting off of a woman's hand (Deut 25:11-12). As contemporary Christians read and ponder the biblical instructions pertaining to the rod, the whip and the heavy knife, they are likely to struggle with what they find.

If I am the only person in the world who is troubled by the corporal punishment texts in the Bible, then I might as well climb into a sound-proof room and from the depths of my lamenting heart read these pages to myself and to God. However, I know from speaking with other Christians that many share the feeling of a troubled soul, and thus my attempt here is to speak to a wider audience about the issues that cause this spiritual disquiet. After hearing two contemporary stories, we will turn to Scripture and encounter a difficult reality—an unsettling juxtaposition of values.

TWO STORIES

The first story is about a six-year-old boy whom I have never met. Roughly a month before I finished this book, I came across a news article that described a man in Fredericton, New Brunswick (Canada), being given a forty-five-day jail sentence for spanking his son. As I read the article more closely, it became clear that the man was not being jailed simply for spanking his six-year-old child but for doing so in a manner that left behind bruising marks.[1] Here in Canada, if a parent spanks and leaves bruising welts and marks, Family and Child Services (a government agency) can and often do take children away from the parents. "Leaving marks" corporal punishment is viewed as abusive treatment. The situation is essentially no different in the United States, Europe and other Western countries. While Christians today might debate the length of the jail sentence or other particulars in this case, one conclusion is broadly shared among present-day believers. Almost all Christians—even pro-spankers today—view the leaving of marks as an abusive parenting action. We are saddened when we read about a six-year-old having been beaten by his father in this fashion.

The second story is a lot closer to home for me. It is a story about a young man named Fanosie—a former Ethiopian student of mine who is extremely bright and possesses a warm and inspiring pastoral heart.[2] Over his time as an M.Div. student we became very good friends, and Marilyn and I enjoyed getting to know Fanosie and his wife in various contexts—our home, their home, local Ethiopian restaurants and campus discussions. After gentle arm twisting by Fanosie, a couple of summers ago I went to teach for a month in two Ethiopian evangelical seminaries—one seminary right in the capital city of Addis Ababa and one seminary just to the south of Addis, about one hour's travel, with the wildest highway driving I have ever experienced.

As I was preparing for the Ethiopia trip, I gave Fanosie several chapters of this book on corporal punishment, asking for his feedback. More specifically, I asked if I should take this material to Addis and teach some of it there. About a week or two later, I bumped into Fanosie in the foyer of our seminary and asked him what he thought about the chapters. I still remember his vivid answer. He said nothing, nothing at all. Instead, Fanosie bent down his head and showed me a series of welts, scars and ugly disfigurations. He is tall man and his dark curly

---

[1]"N.B. Man Jailed for Spanking Son," *CBC News*, February 2, 2010. The article can be accessed at <www.cbc.ca/news/canada/new-brunswick/story/2010/02/02/nb-spanking-sentencing.html>.
[2]This story has been cited with Fanosie's written consent.

hair hid these marks fairly well. He explained to me that he could take off his clothes and show me more marks from beatings he had as a child. He described being raised in a typical Christian home, and how, not infrequently, his father beat him with a stick. In fact, Fanosie told how it was still acceptable for many Christian husbands in Ethiopia to beat their wives as an act of corrective discipline. I stood there shocked and unable to speak. When I found my voice again, I said to Fanosie, "I am not sure I know exactly what you are telling me. Are you saying this topic is going to be too explosive and I should not take these chapters?" He looked at me and said, "No. You *must* teach this in Ethiopia!" In addition to the seminary classes on biblical interpretation that I had lined up for weekdays, Fanosie arranged a three-hour Saturday morning session for Ethiopian pastors and church leaders along with seminary students and local professors. The topic he chose for this widest audience was from the pages contained in this book. I will never forget that Saturday morning.[3] Suffice it to say that the topic addressed a keenly felt need as Fanosie had anticipated.

But there is something far more important for us to focus on. We must now connect these two stories to the Bible. We need to relate the marks and bruises left from physical beatings of the Fredericton child and of Fanosie to what is taught in Scripture about corporal punishment.

TURNING TO SCRIPTURE

Here is how a troubled soul arises. On the one hand, I feel angry and upset about what happened to the young Fredericton boy. And I feel outraged about what my friend Fanosie experienced in his home. I ask myself, *What sort of parents would discipline their kids so that they leave these*

---

[3]After the closing prayer, my son (Joel) and I were literally mobbed for a few handouts that I left up front for those who might be interested in further reading. Due to the audience pressing for this pile of handouts and some wanting to talk with us, we virtually could not move for several minutes. At the moment I stood there and thought, "Well, of course photocopying is expensive in Ethiopia and maybe there are other cultural components that I do not understand." However, several people later explained that this response was not typical for such a Christian leadership gathering held in a seminary campus setting. As Fanosie had anticipated, the topic had clearly hit a nerve. The audience was eager to think through a different approach to applying the Bible in this area of corporal punishment.

kinds of bruises and markings? This sort of corporal punishment is wrong and abusive. But then I turn to the pages of Scripture and discover something that greatly troubles my Christian soul. It leaves me shaking my head and confused about the God I believe in and cherish. Rather than being strengthened in my faith, I am puzzled and disturbed.

I discover that the Bible does not view the leaving of marks and bruises from a beating as abusive. Instead of seeing them as deplorable, the Bible regards them as a virtue in that they signify a good and effective beating. In the first chapter on "seven ways" we will look at one biblical proverb (Prov 20:30) that teaches this perspective on physical beatings. Since the recipient of the beating in Proverbs 20:30 is not explicitly described (whether adult or child), I would like to think that this biblical text is talking about adult beatings and not about the beating of children. This would alleviate at least *some* of the ethical tension. Alas, I fear that such a limited, adult-only understanding of the biblical proverb is wishful thinking on my part. I will explain why in the first chapter.

Although I am taught within Scripture that marks from physical beatings are a virtue, somehow I cannot tear myself away from what I have always held, namely, that such actions are abusive. But the struggle only begins here. This one troubling component within the corporal punishment texts in the Bible is just a start. There is much more that is ethically problematic. We will explore a range of biblical teaching about the rod and whip (chap. 1) and about the heavy knife (chap. 4) that should cause us to rethink how we move from ancient biblical texts to an application of those texts for today.

A BOOK ABOUT HERMENEUTICS

Let me warn you that this is *not* a book about parenting techniques. If you want a limited discussion of parenting practices related to discipline, I have included a postscript called "An Unplanned Parenting Journey." (Readers interested primarily in the perplexing hermeneutical questions can skip that material if they wish.) Rather, this book is about how to read and understand the Bible. The book captures the *hermeneutical* journey of Marilyn (my wife) and me as we have raised our three children. We did not see it coming. We did not in any way anticipate this "reading Scripture" pilgrimage in our lives as parents. It was quite literally an unplanned journey about how to interpret and apply Scripture.

Let me describe our hermeneutical journey this way—it was as if we were walking backward, stumbling along in the dark and quite by accident we started bumping into the findings of this book. To be sure, we *thought* we were disciplining our children in a manner that was taught in Scripture. But much to our surprise we discovered that the spanking-type discipline we were practicing had very little correlation to what the Bible actually taught about corporal punishment. To our further dismay, as we began digging into the teaching of Scripture on corporal punishment (the rod, the whip and the heavy knife), we discovered various texts and biblical instructions that were deeply disturbing. The corporal punishment passages in the Bible indeed began to trouble our Christian souls.

For a brief moment, let me jump ahead to say that our "reading Scripture" journey does not end the same way it began. It starts with troubled souls but ends on a much happier note. Along the pathway we encountered a new (well, new for us) way of understanding Scripture. We discovered something called a "redemptive movement" approach to reading and applying the Bible. This was a much better way of thinking about how we should live out the Bible than what we had practiced before, and it has helped us come to terms with, and not simply overlook, some of the disturbing ethical components within the biblical portrait. We were able to make peace with what we had found so unsettling on the sacred page. Most importantly, a redemptive-movement approach to reading the Bible helped us to think more clearly about what God desired from us as parents.

In short, this book offers a case study within the corporal punishment texts about how Christians ought to interpret and apply Scripture. I will argue for reading Scripture with a redemptive-movement hermeneutic. Chapter two explains what is meant by a redemptive-movement hermeneutic and illustrates its usage in the slavery texts of the Bible. As you will come to see, a redemptive-movement hermeneutic is not entirely new at all. It merely takes what we typically do in interpreting Scripture and enables us to do it a little better. A redemptive-movement hermeneutic fits as a subcomponent within a standard and well-accepted grammatical-historical approach, particularly in its emphasis on reading biblical texts within their ancient historical context. I will propose that by adding a redemptive-movement component to classic grammatical-historical hermeneutics, we significantly strengthen our grammatical-historical method. It does a far better job of the "historical" side of the grammatical-historical approach. Along strictly hermeneutical lines, then, the central question of the book could be posed this way: *Should Christians using a grammatical-historical hermeneutic add (or not add) a component of redemptive-movement meaning and application as they read the corporal punishment texts?*

So, here is our story—our stumbling, bumbling, parenting story—as at it relates to the *hermeneutics* of reading and applying Scripture. I hope that you will in some measure be able to travel with us on a biblical journey that reflects upon the rod, the whip and the heavy knife. But let us go back and start at the beginning of our hermeneutical pilgrimage with the opening chapter. Our journey began with first discovering some unsettling and downright disturbing components to the corporal punishment instructions within the Bible.

PART I

Troubling Texts

1

BIBLICAL TEXTS,
ETHICAL DILEMMAS AND
HERMENEUTICAL INCONSISTENCIES

Christian advocates of spanking generally claim that their practices have the backing of Scripture, and thus God's approval. They view the Bible and its instructions about corporal punishment as a solid basis for their disciplinary methods. The most notable spokesperson for corporal punishment in the evangelical Christian context is James Dobson and the Focus on the Family organization.[1] Along with others, Dobson presents his teachings about spanking as rooted in the Bible. True biblical obedience means daring to follow God's instructions about corporal punishment of one's children.[2]

At the outset of this discussion let me clearly say that I am not at odds in any polarized or hostile sense with Dobson's "two-smacks-

---

[1] James Dobson was the founder and longtime CEO of Focus on the Family ministries. On February 26, 2010, Dobson gave his last radio broadcast with Focus on the Family and has been succeeded by Jim Daly as president of the organization. This leadership shift has brought some changes to Focus on the Family, but their endorsement of corporal punishment for children remains the same. They continue to recommend Dobson's materials on their website under various discussions of corporal punishment/spanking. A few recent changes in their teachings about spanking will be noted in certain footnotes within this chapter.

[2] James Dobson, *The New Dare to Discipline*, 2nd ed. (Carol Stream, Ill.: Tyndale House, 1992). Between the book's first edition (1970) and its present updated form (1992) more than 3,500,000 copies have been sold. Of particular interest is the reference in the second edition to Dobson's methods not needing to change from the first edition because children have not changed and his spanking method is derived from the "inspired concepts of Scripture" (p. 4). Seemingly, Dobson's point is that corporal punishment, as developed within his two-edition book, has the backing of the Bible and its authority.

max" approach to disciplining children. While we ultimately differ in methods, it is not his method itself that I find most troubling. In fact, I really like where he has come over the years in his development of a restrained two-smacks-max method.[3] Our differences in disciplinary methods for raising children are important but secondary to the larger hermeneutical issues about how Christians derive their ethic from Scripture.

So, what is the crucial hermeneutical issue? What I find most problematic is the appeal by Christian pro-spankers to the Bible in order to validate their corporal punishment practices. In short, Christian pro-spankers claim that they have the Bible on their side. The Bible clearly teaches corporal punishment, they say, and thus their instructions about spanking children are biblical. As typical of this concrete-specific approach, Wayne Grudem argues from the instruction of Scripture that there really is no other "biblical position" than for Christian parents to support the use of corporal punishment in society and to use corporal punishment in the discipline of their children.[4] For a Christian parent to do otherwise is in some way to undermine biblical authority. At one point I held this perspective. I actually taught this view to theological students and to pastors. What I have discovered, however, is that I was wrong. It is not an overstatement to say that this hermeneutical journey has left me surprised and even dumbfounded at times. I came to realize that at the level of concrete-specific instructions in Scripture, my beloved two-smacks-max parenting method had very little correlation to what the Bible actually teaches about corporal punishment.

I promise to walk gently down the corridors of Focus on the Family, because it functions as a valuable family support ministry for the church. We in theological academia (seminary professors) must shoulder the greater responsibility for the current confusion about how to read and apply Scripture. Thus while citing Focus on the Family and Dobson in

---

[3]I do not know if Dobson ever labels his method "two-smacks-max" or "two-spanks-max." I have done so because it provides a memorable way of highlighting a very positive component of restraint within his approach.

[4]Wayne A. Grudem, *Politics According to the Bible: A Comprehensive Resource for Understanding Modern Political Issues in Light of Scripture* (Grand Rapids: Zondervan, 2010), pp. 256-60.

this chapter, my strongest disagreements lie with biblical scholars such as Andreas Köstenberger, Al Mohler, Wayne Grudem and Paul Wegner, who have recently published on this subject. They cite the classic "beating with the rod" texts from Proverbs in order to derive a biblical mandate for parents to spank their children today:

> Those who spare the rod hate their children,
>> but those who love them are diligent to discipline them.
>>> (Prov 13:24)

> Folly is bound up in the heart of a boy,
>> but the rod of discipline drives it far away. (Prov 22:15)

> Do not withhold discipline from your children;
>> if you beat them with a rod, they will not die.
> If you beat them with the rod,
>> you will save their lives from Sheol [the grave or premature death].
>>> (Prov 23:13-14)

> The rod and reproof give wisdom,
>> but a mother is disgraced by a neglected child.
>>> (Prov 29:15; cf. Prov 19:18; 29:17)

Upon reading these proverbs Christian parents are easily persuaded about the pro-spankers' claim that the spanking of children today is indeed biblical and even necessary.

After placing the weight of responsibility on Christian academia, let me temper any combative posture with an embarrassing confession. I used to cite these Proverbs as support for spanking in exactly the same way as Köstenberger, Mohler, Grudem, Wegner and others do. I cannot give them a hard time over the way that they handle these texts. In a sense, my disagreement is not with them at all. It is with me—my former self! I am the one who has severely mishandled these texts over the years without being the least bit aware of it. I have slowly come to understand the degree to which I was not really teaching or following the Bible with my two-smacks-max pro-spanking methods. To a large extent, I and others have forgotten to read the rod and whip texts within the broader biblical teaching about corporal punishment. We have also forgotten to understand and appreciate them within the horizon of the ancient Near Eastern world. Accordingly, this chapter walks through ways that I was blind to much that the Bible teaches about corporal punishment. While I will cite various Christian scholars on the pro-spanking side for illustration's sake, a number of years ago I could easily have written their materials.

Over the years the pro-spanking Christian community has unwittingly moved beyond the Bible and its concrete-specific teachings about the rod and whip. This chapter outlines the seven ways. To peek ahead, however, chapters two and three will argue that the pro-spankers' movement beyond the Bible's concrete-specific teaching is actually is a good thing. I truly think that they have moved beyond the Bible *biblically*. I suspect that this redemptive movement or ethical development is for many rooted in an intuitive sense of moral and ethical virtue. It is the mind of Christ, as Paul would say, functioning within the church community. But I am getting ahead of myself. I jumped ahead with a glimpse of what is coming only so that you will not be overly harsh in your opinion of these pro-spankers for *not* doing what the Bible clearly teaches. In five of the examples today's pro-spankers have chosen to disregard an *explicit* teaching of Scripture; in two examples they disregard an *implicit* teaching of Scripture. Nevertheless, whether it is explicit or implicit teaching on corporal punishment, at a concrete-specific level today's pro-spankers (and I was one of them) are not doing what the Bible teaches in its fuller discussion of the subject.

Here are the seven ways that pro-spankers go beyond the specific teachings about corporal punishment found in the Bible: (1) age limitations, (2) the number of lashes or strokes, (3) the bodily location of the beating, (4) the resultant bruising, welts and wounds, (5) the instrument of discipline, (6) the frequency of beatings and offenses punishable, and (7) the emotive disposition of the parent. We will examine each of these.

AGE LIMITATIONS

Christian advocates for spanking today generally place an upper age limit somewhere around ten years. Wegner states that spanking should decrease at age six and be rarely, if ever, used beyond age ten.[5] According to Köstenberger spanking may not work well with older children, and as children advance in age, reasoning ought to replace spanking.[6] Focus on the Family provides similar age-restricted guidelines: spanking works best between ages two and six; most spanking should occur during preschool years and become less and less frequent, tapering off completely between age nine and twelve; no spanking teenagers.[7]

Do age limits on spanking really reflect what the Bible teaches about corporal punishment? No, I do not think so. We can invoke age restrictions on spanking only if a handful of Proverbs texts are taken out of the broader teaching in the Bible about corporal punishment. Once dislodged from their biblical moorings, this package of Proverbs often is blessed by citing Hebrews 12 about a loving God disciplining his children, and then we are set to introduce any sort of age-restricted physical discipline we

---

[5]Paul D. Wegner, "Discipline in the Book of Proverbs: 'To Spank or Not to Spank,'" *Journal of the Evangelical Theological Society* 48, no. 4 (2005): 732. Wegner cites the Family Research Council for support of this view.

[6]Andreas J. Köstenberger with David W. Jones, *God, Marriage and Family: Rebuilding the Biblical Foundation* (Wheaton, Ill.: Crossway, 2004), p. 161.

[7]Focus on the Family, "Age-Appropriate Discipline," accessed February 7, 2010, <www.focuso nyourchild.com/develop/art1/A0000188.html>. Although this URL is not currently accessible, an archived version is available at <http://replay.waybackmachine.org/20071006063619/ http://focusonyourchild.com/develop/art1/A0000188.html>.

While Focus on the Family still endorses corporal punishment and recommends Dobson's books, they have clearly moved to limiting spanking from the age of nineteen months to age five, max (spanking is only for *pre*-elementary years). In the past, Focus on the Family encouraged a tapering off of spanking during elementary years and none for teens. Now they recommend spanking only for children age five and under and none for elementary-age children or for teens. In contrast with Scripture, which clearly teaches the effectiveness of corporal punishment for both elementary-age children and teenagers, Focus on the Family teaches that spanking is not effective past age five. See the more recent website links: Focus on the Family, "Does Spanking Cause Kids to Become Violent?" published April 14, 2010, <http://family.custhelp .com/app/answers/detail/a_id/25648/~/does-spanking-cause-kids-to-become-violent%3F>. Cf. Focus on the Family, "Can You Provide Me with Some General Principles and Guidelines for Disciplining My Elementary School Child?" published July 26, 2010, modified December 1, 2010, <http://family.custhelp.com/app/answers/detail/a_id/25943/kw/spanking>. In the latter article on general guidelines, the general ineffectiveness of elementary-age spanking is clearly taught: "Remember that, for the most part, spankings don't work very well at this stage [elementary years] in a child's development, and that their ineffectiveness can actually escalate the situation and lead to abuse." This Focus on the Family perspective contradicts the explicit teaching of the Bible with respect to (a) *age limits* and (b) the *effectiveness* of corporal punishment for elementary-age children and teens.

want. Unfortunately, this highly modified spanking version of the rod passages today does not reflect Scripture's face-value teaching or concrete-specific instruction about corporal punishment.

So what are the Bible's age limits on corporal punishment? Based on the concrete-specific teachings of the Bible, the answer quite simply is there are none! That's right. There are no age limits. The instructions for beating children in Scripture do not stand alone; they intersect with at least three other spheres of corporal punishment: slaves, fools and Torah violators. For each of these categories the adult application of the rod or whip was a normative biblical virtue. The Deuteronomy text that establishes physical beatings as a broad-based punishment for Torah infractions (Deut 25:1-3) was in all likelihood applied as early as twelve to fourteen years of age.[8] The Exodus text that supports beating slaves (Ex 21:20-21) may well have applied to all slaves regardless of their age.[9] The verses in Proverbs that encourage the use of corporal punishment for fools seem to have a fairly broad referent that may have at times included both adults and children. At the very least there would be a tacit aspect of referential overlap because the child-discipline texts emphasize the curbing of "foolishness," which would tie them conceptually with the texts about "beating fools" (Prov 10:13; 18:6; 19:29; 26:3).[10] Given this larger biblical context, the idea of primarily spanking preschoolers, tapering off from there and eliminating all spankings for teenagers, while appearing reasonable to contemporary readers, is simply not biblical at the level of what the Bible explicitly teaches.

Along these lines, the overlap in purpose or function makes age

---

[8]Within Scripture the transition to adulthood appears to be around age twelve to fourteen; within our present-day world that transition happens somewhat later between eighteen and twenty-one years. This difference would create a slightly more gradual progression in today's context in moving toward the forty maximum lashes. Nevertheless, it does not change the basic point about physical beatings for teens being a biblical concept in the sense that it is part of the Bible's concrete-specific instructions.

[9]There is no explicit age restriction within this slavery text, and its intent to protect the life of the slave would clearly be applicable to younger slaves (children). Since admonitions within Scripture to beat children do not differentiate between slave or free children, it makes sense that at times a slave owner may well have beaten child-aged slaves. If so, Ex 21:20-21 would seem to have even greater relevance to children (than to adult slaves) given the greater vulnerability of their smaller, less-developed bodies.

[10]The overlap in functional language, as developed later in this chapter, would support a broader referent in the texts addressing fools or at least a second level of applicability.

limitations rather inappropriate. Notice that the negative purpose of "driving out foolishness" in the child text of Proverbs 22:15 is the same virtue that appears across a much broader age spectrum of verses about corporal punishment:

Child

Folly is bound up in the heart of a boy,
>but the rod of discipline drives it [namely, *foolishness*] far away.
>>(Prov 22:15)

Adult

A fool's lips bring strife,
>and a fool's mouth invites a flogging. (Prov 18:6)

Condemnation is ready for scoffers,
>and flogging for the backs of fools. (Prov 19:29)

A whip for the horse, a bridle for the donkey,
>and a rod for the back of fools. (Prov 26:3; cf. Prov 10:13)

If beatings get rid of foolishness in both children and adults, why stop at any age?

Correspondingly, the positive purpose of encouraging wisdom, obedience and knowledge is a shared virtue that fuses together the *child* texts of Proverbs (and the ancient Jewish writing, Wisdom of Sirach)[11] with other biblical texts directed toward *adult* slaves and fools:

Child

The rod and reproof give wisdom,
>but a mother is disgraced by a neglected child. (Prov 29:15)

Bow down his neck in his youth,
>and beat his sides while he is young,
or else he will become stubborn and disobey you,
>and you will have sorrow of soul from him. (Sir 30:12)

---

[11]While not considered Scripture by most Protestants, the Wisdom of Sirach (c. 200 B.C.E.) is included as a deuterocanonical book in Roman Catholic, Greek and Slavonic Bibles. Furthermore, the book is an example of ancient Jewish literature and thus extremely valuable for learning how ancient readers understood the biblical text. Both Köstenberger and Wegner include references to Wisdom of Sirach in their discussions of biblical discipline.

Adult

By mere words servants are not disciplined,
> for though they understand, they will not give heed [will not be
> obedient]. (Prov 29:19)

Strike [beat] a scoffer, and the simple will learn prudence;
> reprove the intelligent, and they will gain knowledge. (Prov 19:25)

In view of this overlap in functional language, the Bible unquestionably teaches that teenagers would benefit from beatings or lashes for the purpose of driving out foolishness and building up wisdom and knowledge. Against the grain of pro-spankers today who have abandoned corporal punishment for teenagers, on a concrete-specific teaching level the Bible says it is helpful! One *might* be inclined to go with the Bible here (please bear with my hypothetical critique) if for no other reason than what is obvious about teenagers. While at times they evidence maturity beyond their years, it is also the case that teens frequently give the term *foolishness* a whole new range of colorful meanings. One might say that teenagers at times specialize in foolishness! Given the larger context of scriptural teaching on corporal punishment and its overlapping purposes that span all ages, the biblical admonition to today's parents is clear: teenagers need foolishness driven out by the rod during these wild and wooly years just as much as, if not more than, in earlier phases of their development.

Of course, my point here is not really a critique of contemporary two-smacks-max child discipline practices. At the level of praxis I agree with them on how they are handling teenagers—I think it is a good thing *not* to spank teenagers and older elementary age children within today's world. The real issue that I am wrestling with in this chapter is this—What then does it mean to be biblical in our contemporary application of Scripture? Please understand that I am interacting with the perspective of those who typically see their corporal punishment practices as "biblical" when they do what is reflected in the concrete-specific teaching of the biblical text. In other words, if the Bible teaches physical beatings or spankings for children, then Christians ought to do just that. Yet, they have clearly abandoned the instruction of Scripture they claim to be following when it comes to disciplinary beatings for older children and teenagers.

One final thought about today's (artificial) age limits. What about Deuteronomy 21:18-21, which advocates the stoning of a severely rebellious teenager? It makes little sense to create a Grand Canyon-sized gap of no spanking teenagers when by virtue of severe rebellion, a teenager might wind up being stoned by the community. Don't the Proverbs say something about "applying the rod in order to save the child from Sheol [premature death]" (Prov 23:14; cf. Prov 19:18)? Of course, an understanding of "premature death" could encompass many things. But a biblical theology of corporal punishment sees the rod and whip in a teen's life as a necessary intervening and preventative step in order to avoid the more dreadful outcome of death by stoning.[12] It is hardly reasonable to read our Bibles as saying, "Abandon the rod for teenagers who are mildly or moderately rebellious, but go ahead and stone them if they get to the point of severe rebellion." The rod and whip instructions must be placed within the broader biblical spectrum of correctives for teenagers.

NUMBER OF LASHES OR STROKES

Today's pro-spanking Christians place an upper limit on the number of times a parent should hit the child—the maximum number is two. No more than two smacks on the bottom are permitted.[13] Wegner endorses the perspective of the Family Research Council and so writes, "A single slap to the hand of a young child, and one or two spanks to the buttocks for older children are recommended amounts."[14] Similarly, Focus on the Family places a cap on the number of spanks at two but adds a scaling strategy that reserves a single spank for lesser infractions and two spanks for greater infractions.[15]

---

[12]Even Wegner draws a connection between the "avoiding death" discipline texts of Proverbs and the stoning text of Deut 21:18-21 ("Discipline in the Book of Proverbs," p. 728).

[13]Focus on the Family, "Does Spanking Cause Kids to Become Violent?" Cf. Dobson, *New Dare to Discipline*, p. 65.

[14]See Wegner, "Discipline in the Book of Proverbs," p. 732.

[15]The Focus website taught this differentiation between one smack for minor infractions and two for major infractions in an article titled "Discipline From Ages 4 to 8," Focus on the Family, <http://focusonyourchild.com/introduction/imageintro/A0001664.html>, accessed Feb-

We must ask whether this "no more than two smacks" limit on physi-cal discipline correctly represents the Bible's concrete-specific teachings. Once again, the answer is no. Within a broader theology of corporal punishment the maximum limit on strokes or lashes is clearly set at forty (not two) strokes for Torah infractions (Deut 25:3). True, this maximum limit of forty strokes or lashes is applied to adults or at least to those within the covenant community considered old enough to be responsible for Torah obedience. In all likelihood within Israel, forty lashes would be the maximum limit for teenagers as well as for older adults.[16]

So what about children in the preteen years? Does it make sense within a biblical framework that the maximum strokes with a rod or whip would be only *two* for children but then the number jumps up to *forty* upon reaching the teen years? This is hardly a logical way of reading or applying Scripture. It would be more convincing to under-stand the biblical paradigm within some kind of gradual or graded movement toward the maximum of forty lashes. For instance, let's spread those lashes or strokes over twelve years in a proportional way starting at age two. This would give us roughly a variance of four ad-ditional lashes per each year. This progression would blend seamlessly with the forty maximum by the time children became teenagers. Once again, if teenagers are old enough to die by stoning for their extreme rebellion, then surely they are old enough for the maximum strokes of corporal punishment.

---

ruary 7, 2010. Since the upper age limit on spanking for the next generation or the post-Dobson Focus on the Family is now five years old (and an even smaller "preferred" window of use between ages two and three-and-a-half years old), this former webpage is no longer avail-able and has obviously been changed to reflect new thought. Nevertheless, the number of smacks is still a maximum of two, and it would seem reasonable to infer that a continued use of scaling depends on the nature of the infraction (but I could not find this explicitly stated). See Focus on the Family, "Does Spanking Cause Kids to Become Violent?"

[16]For sake of clarity I will generally reserve the modern terms *spanking* and *smacks* for the present-day phenomenon of Christian corporal punishment, which has radically departed from the biblical portrait of "beatings with the rod" or "floggings with the whip." I am not attempting to be inflammatory with my language. I am simply adding a dose of interpretive realism and trying to read the so-called spanking texts as a part of a broader theology and practice of corporal punishment within Scripture. For instance, the rod and whip are the same instruments used in the corporal punishment of slaves and free adults. It would be silly to talk about Israelite masters spanking their slaves or of the Jewish authorities administering "forty spankings less one" to the apostle (Ex 21:20-21; 2 Cor 11:24).

BODILY LOCATION OF THE BEATINGS

Pro-spanking evangelicals today argue that the best bodily location for physical discipline is either the hand or the buttocks. Wegner advocates a "single slap to the *hand* of a young child, and one or two spanks to the *buttocks* for older children."[17] In a Focus on the Family Q&A document Dobson answers the question about bodily location in a similar fashion: "It [spanking] should be confined to the buttocks area, where permanent damage is very unlikely."[18] Given the consideration about damaging a child, the buttocks seem to have won out as the preferred location among Christian pro-spankers.

However, is this bottom-spanking tradition truly biblical? If we are talking about the concrete instructions of the Bible, the answer once again is no. The broader thematic discussion of Scripture lays out exactly where on the body such beatings are to be administered. Within the text of Deuteronomy, God instructs judges that they "shall make that person [a Torah violator] lie down and be beaten in his presence" (Deut 25:2). This positioning gave the person with the rod or whip a height advantage in order to deliver strong blows to the offender's back.[19] Of course, lashes on the back would often curl around to the sides as well. Accordingly, Scripture and other ancient Jewish literature speak positively of beatings administered to the person's back or sides:[20]

Fool

On the lips of one who has understanding wisdom is found,
　　but a rod is for the *back* of one who lacks sense. (Prov 10:13)

Condemnation is ready for scoffers,
　　and flogging for the *backs* of fools. (Prov 19:29)

A whip for the horse, a bridle for the donkey,
　　and a rod for the *back* of fools. (Prov 26:3)

---

[17]Wegner, "Discipline in the Book of Proverbs," p. 732, italics added.

[18]See Focus on the Family, "Does Spanking Cause Kids to Become Violent?" Cf. Dobson, *New Dare to Discipline*, p. 63.

[19]While the text of Deuteronomy does not explicitly say to "beat the back", this is the most likely bodily location conveyed by the instructions in view of the broad coverage of lashes with a whip.

[20]To this list I could add the theological example from Josh 23:13, "The LORD your God [will use the nations . . .] they shall be . . . a scourge on your *sides*."

Servant
I [the servant] gave my *back* to those who struck [beat] me.
  (Is 50:6)

Child
Bow down his neck in his youth,
    and *beat his sides* while he is young,
or else he will become stubborn and disobey you,
    and you will have sorrow of soul from him. (Sir 30:12)

As with the foundational Torah-violator text of Deuteronomy, flog-gings on the back or sides are carried out within each of the other three categories: fools, slaves and children. While the explicit child example comes from the Wisdom of Sirach, the other "backs of fools" proverbs may have a broad referent that, beyond adults, would likely have in-cluded children, especially in view of the fact that folly was bound up in the heart of the child and was to be driven out by beatings with a rod. It is hard to separate the fool-beating texts of Proverbs from what is said about disciplining children. Thus the biblical location for beatings is clearly the back and not the buttocks for Torah breakers, fools, servants and most likely children.[21]

Obviously contemporary spanking advocates have moved away from flogging the back to spanking the buttocks. At first glance this change may seem trivial. But this is not so. The reason that pro-spankers have moved to spanking on the buttocks (contrary to the Bible's concrete and specific instructions) is important: it is the one physical location where permanent damage is most unlikely.[22] In other words, the change is one advanced by Christian pediatricians and biblical scholars who know full well that beatings across the back and sides can injure internal organs (e.g., kidneys). The change from back

---

[21]The beating of children/youth on the back was common ANE practice as in the Egyptian schoolbook *Papyrus Lansing*: "I grew into a youth at your side. You beat my back; your teaching entered my ear" (Miriam Lichtheim, *Ancient Egyptian Literature: A Book of Readings* [Berkeley: University of California Press, 1973-1980], 2:172). Cf. the Papyrus Anastasi III, "A boy's ear is upon his back, he hearkens to his beater," as cited by Bruce K. Waltke, *Book of Proverbs: Chapters 1-15*, NICOT (Grand Rapids: Eerdmans, 2004), p. 574 n. 116.

[22]This change for the better also corresponds to the departure from the whip, which would not be controlled as well in terms of an isolated, smaller bodily location.

to buttocks is not a minor one. It represents a much-improved practice of discipline beyond what is found in the Bible (at least in terms of its concrete instructions).

The movement away from biblical instructions and proverbial wisdom about "the backs of fools" is not a simple swapping of ancient and modern equivalents. A marked improvement has been made. The developed ethic of evangelical spanking advocates has in fact gone beyond the Bible to what I will later describe (chaps. 2-3) as a greater fulfillment of the Bible's redemptive spirit. They have taken the redemptive spirit, which resides within the corporal punishment texts themselves, and gone beyond the concrete, frozen-in-time particulars of the text to a fuller realization of the biblical ethic. Most Christian spanking advocates, while appealing with all sincerity to the Bible for what they practice, seem oblivious to the hermeneutical move they make in arriving at their present-day spanking practices. I include my own blindness and slow-moving journey here as well.

RESULTANT BRUISES, WELTS AND WOUNDS

Christian advocates for spanking today maintain that their loving use of corporal punishment is not abusive. This asserted value—"we are not abusive in our treatment of children"—is demonstrated in the loving disposition of the parent, the restricted number of hits (two-smacks-max) and the nonabusive spanking dictum: "Do not leave any marks." None of the prominent spokespersons cited would say it is an accepted part of their spanking practices to leave bruising or welts on a child. They would argue strenuously against this kind of abusive treatment of children. They would want to distance themselves from any bizarre "Christian cult groups," as Wegner puts it, that discipline children in such a way as to leave physical welts, bruises or cuts.[23] Any physical marks or bruising that result from corporal punishment is considered by these Christian pro-spankers to be unacceptable and deplorable.[24] They do not mince words about what constitutes physical abuse. They

---

[23]See Wegner, "Discipline in the Book of Proverbs," pp. 726-27, esp. n. 56.

[24]Focus on the Family teaches that "spanking should never be done in such a way as to bruise a child." See Focus on the Family, "Does Spanking Cause Kids to Become Violent?"

would be just as distraught as I was (and am) over what recently happened to a six-year-old Fredericton boy and over what happened a few years ago to my Ethiopian friend Fanosie (see the introduction).

I admire such a vigorous campaign for nonabusive corporal punishment—physical discipline that leaves no bruises, welts or wounds. My only problem with the "no bruising" position is that it contradicts concrete-specific biblical teaching on corporal punishment. If we root contemporary spanking practices in the concrete teachings of the Bible, then the "spanking without bruising" approach ultimately results in the Christian appearing to live in disobedience to Scripture. A larger survey of corporal punishment texts within the Bible does not draw the boundary line where these contemporary pro-spankers want to put it. Instead, the very clear demarcation regarding beatings in the Bible is that, as in the case of a slave, the recipient (1) must not be killed, (2) must not have any permanent physical injury or dismemberment, and (3) must be able to get up a day or two after the beating (Ex 21:20-21, 26-27). Aside from these three limitations for slaves and (4) the limitation of forty strokes for free people guilty of Torah infractions (Deut 25:3), the concept of "leaving no marks" is foreign to the Bible. Rather, the bruises that come from beatings are seen as a virtue.

Comparing Proverbs 22:15 to Proverbs 20:30, we begin to see how "beating children with the rod" texts are tied thematically to other biblical texts that speak about beatings that leave marks. Just as the rod drives away foolishness from children, the Proverbs speak in a similar positive fashion about the bruises that come from such blows as the means for cleansing away evil.

> Folly is bound up in the heart of a boy,
>> but the rod of discipline drives it [foolishness] far away. (Prov 22:15)

> Blows that wound [or bruise] cleanse away evil;
>> beatings make clean the innermost parts. (Prov 20:30)

These two proverbs celebrate a shared benefit or purpose that beatings drive (or cleanse) away folly and evil.[25] In Proverbs 20:30 the re-

---

[25]Consider also the interesting parallel between bruises from beatings and cleansing from sin in Sir 23:10.

cipient of the beating is unstated; it seems to have a broad referent that would include Torah violators, slaves, fools and children. The focus in 20:30 simply makes explicit the well-known outcome of beatings within the ancient world, namely, that they often bruised or wounded the recipient regardless of age. There is a striking interconnectedness in thought between these two proverbs. Keeping them clinically separated in our application, as today's spanking advocates do,[26] amounts to a modern-day imposition upon the Bible.[27]

Within a biblical theology of beatings, any temporary bruising, welts or wounds—at least ones that could heal over time—were an accepted and approved part of corporal punishment. This should be obvious from the slavery text of Exodus 21:20-21, where the severity of a beating is limited only by the requirement that the slave could physically get up after a day or two. Thus biblical teaching about beatings is that the slave's welts, bruises and potentially bleeding wounds could be severe. It was acceptable for those wounds to take a couple of days not necessarily even to heal completely (that might take longer), but to be sufficiently attended to and on the way to mending so that the slave could at least start moving around.

Other biblical passages and extrabiblical ones, including ancient Jewish texts (e.g., the Wisdom of Sirach) further establish the fact that beatings would frequently leave some kind of temporary physical damage. These welts and wounds were not viewed as shameful or abusive action on the part of the one administering the beating; they were seen as a good and reasonable thing within the practice of corporal punishment. The examples below provide evidence that beatings frequently resulted in "black mark" bruising, welts and possibly even bleeding wounds. Interestingly, the evidence cuts across both the human and theological domain:[28]

---

[26]See Wegner, "Discipline in the Book of Proverbs," p. 726.

[27]Many scholars place Prov 20:30 within a grouping of proverbs that address beatings with the rod in the home/child setting and view it as part of the sage's repeated endorsement of corporal punishment. See R. E. Clements, *Wisdom in Theology* (Grand Rapids: Eerdmans, 1992), pp. 138-40; Christine Roy Yoder, *Proverbs*, AOTC (Nashville: Abingdon, 2009), p. 215; James L. Crenshaw, *Old Testament Wisdom: An Introduction* (Louisville: Westminster John Knox, 1998), p. 69; and Tremper Longman III, *Proverbs*, BCOTWP (Grand Rapids: Baker, 2006), p. 386.

[28]"While the old man's eyes were raised to heaven, his flesh was being torn by *scourges*, his *blood*

Literal Human Examples

A servant who is constantly under scrutiny will not lack bruises
   [or "black marks" (KJV) from beatings],
so also the person who always swears and utters the Name will never
   be cleansed from sin. (Sir 23:10)[29]

The blow of a whip raises a welt,
   but a blow of the tongue crushes the bones. (Sir 28:17)

They [the sentinels] beat me, they wounded me, they took away my
   mantle, those sentinels of the walls. (Song 5:7)

And I [Nehemiah] contended with them and cursed them and beat
   some of them and pulled out their hair. (Neh 13:25)[30]

Metaphorical/Theological Examples

The light of the moon will be like the light of the sun . . . on the day
when the LORD binds up the injuries of his people, and heals the
wounds inflicted by his blow [most likely from Yahweh's rod or whip
of discipline].[31] (Is 30:26)

Why do you seek further beatings [from Yahweh's rod or whip]? Why
do you continue to rebel? . . . From the sole of the foot even to the
head, there is no soundness in it, but bruises and sores and bleeding
wounds; they have not been drained, or bound up, or softened with oil.
(Is 1:5-6)[32]

Welts, bruising and wounds were standard fare for biblical beatings by
the rod or whip whether administered literally by human beings or
metaphorically by God upon his people Israel.

    The introduction of theological metaphor, of course, raises impor-
tant questions. I will return to the category of theological analogy

---

flowing, and his sides were being cut to pieces" (4 Macc 6:6). This may well have been an un-
usually harsh beating with non-Jewish instruments. Nevertheless, other texts reflect the standard or typical results of beatings (Acts 16:33; 1 Pet 2:24).

[29]Notice the similar themes about the purifying effects of beating-derived wounds found in Prov
20:30.

[30]While no resultant bodily damage from the "beating" is explicitly stated in Neh 13:25, the
context of physical damages (pulling out people's hair) raises the likelihood that physical
bruising or wounds may well be involved in these beatings.

[31]Cf. Is 10:5, 24-26; 30:31-32; 50:6; 53:5.

[32]Cf. the bruises or wounds of a beaten servant (Is 50:6; 53:5).

below as we discuss the emotive disposition of parents (love but no anger) who administer spankings. At this point, however, permit me to mention briefly a line of reasoning that pro-spankers often adopt. Köstenberger and Wegner, for instance, in part validate their perspective on physical discipline with the argument that God, the perfect Father, disciplines his children (Prov 3:11-12; Heb 12:5-11).[33] They switch between human "beatings with the rod" and divine punishment metaphors with great ease. If God metaphorically disciplines his children with the rod, who are we to reject such a practice? The virtue of beatings with the rod is therefore lauded in the Proverbs and enacted by God himself within theological analogy. It is a powerful pro-spanking argument and nails the case for many Christians simply because they do not understand the dubious nature of ethics based on theological analogy. Unfortunately, the argument is built on a faulty practice of using theological analogy in order to establish contemporary ethics, but without rigorous analysis. This was the very sort of faulty argument that pro-slavery advocates used years ago. I have argued this case and have suggested some guidelines for using theological analogy elsewhere.[34] So, I will refer interested readers to that discussion.

In sum, leaving welts and wounds when using the rod or whip is praised within biblical proverbs (and in extrabiblical Jewish literature), endorsed within other biblical justice texts, and enacted by God within theological metaphor. Who are we today, then, to speak out loudly against leaving bruises or welts and label them "abusive" when in the next breath we claim that our two-smacks-max spanking practices are derived from the Bible? If temporary bodily damage from beatings was good enough for biblical wisdom, for biblical justice and for metaphorical portraits of God himself, then we *could* (I speak hypothetically) argue that surely it ought to be good enough for us to practice today. Of course, I do not believe this type of beating should

---

[33]Köstenberger, *God, Marriage and Family*, pp. 119-20, 161, 384 n. 28; Wegner, "Discipline in the Book of Proverbs," p. 732.

[34]William Webb, *Slaves, Women and Homosexuals* (Downers Grove, Ill.: IVP Academic, 2001), pp. 183-92 (criterion 14).

ever be practiced today with either adults or children. Not for a second. I believe along with Christian pro-spankers today that leaving marks and bruises is abusive and should not be tolerated. But such instruction or teaching within Scripture (and Proverbs no less) should cause us to rethink what exactly we mean when we say that our discipline methods are "biblical."

Pro-spanking advocates for today's "no marks or bruises" corporal punishment might want to raise an objection. Proverbs 20:30 does not explicitly mention children within its endorsement of wounds and bruises as a part of beatings. That is true. However, we must ponder the question of interpretive probability. Which of these options is more probable, the contrastive answer or the continuous answer?

- *Contrastive answer.* The Bible teaches that, *yes*, welts, bruises and wounds are acceptable and even a commendable virtue for adult beatings, but *no*, welts, bruises and wounds are not acceptable when beatings are administered to children; they are deplorable in the case of children and should be considered abusive treatment.

- *Continuous answer.* The Bible teaches that, *yes*, welts, bruises and wounds are acceptable and even commendable for beatings by the rod or whip regardless of age (for the Torah breaker, the fool, the slave and even children) because sound beatings in all of these cases have the effect of driving out folly and evil.

Is the contrastive answer more probable? Or is the continuous answer more likely? Given the ancient-world context of the Bible and its broader teaching about corporal punishment, a contrastive answer does not make much sense. Of course, just as the severity of the infraction sets the number of lashes, so also the age of the person may have tempered the severity of the beating. Nevertheless, a *continuous* answer with incremental increases to account for age is far more likely than a *contrastive* answer.

While I would dearly wish that the Bible taught parents "do not leave marks" on your children when beating them with the rod, it is simply not a compelling way to read Scripture. Unfortunately, we cannot limit Proverbs 20:30—its teaching about the virtue of marks and bruises from beatings—to adults. As already noted, the related material within the Hebrew Bible and within other ancient Jewish wisdom literature makes such an answer highly problematic.

Even more evidence supports a broad-based understanding of Proverbs 20:30, one that would include children within its intended focus. Two further considerations ought to settle the matter. Both call for us to read the "beating children with the rod" texts not within our contemporary world but within the ancient world of the Bible. Here is the first consideration—it highlights the broader biblical context. If within the Bible itself older children could be stoned to death for continual defiance of parents (see previous discussion of Deut 21:18-21), marks and bruises from beatings would hardly have been a concern. In fact, as pointed out earlier in the children texts, beatings ought to be viewed as keeping the child away from such premature death. To think on the level of the concrete instructions that somehow the Bible teaches "marks from beatings are evidence of parental abuse" (our contemporary perspective) merely dislocates the child discipline proverbs from their biblical contextual setting. Furthermore, within the larger biblical picture chopping off of a wife's hand (see chap. 4) must be taken into the mix of what the Bible teaches in the area of corporal punishment. Like it or not, bodily mutilation is a part of an accurate portrayal of biblical corporal punishment. True, this "heavy knife" text, discussed at length in chapter four, involves community-enacted case law and is directed toward a wife (not a child). Nevertheless, it provides the broader brush strokes within which to paint an accurate picture of the range of corporal punishment in the Bible. Given this larger biblical picture, we can assume that no one would have thought twice about leaving marks when beating children with the rod. This is a problem for us today, but not a problem within the Bible.

Here is the second contextual consideration. This consideration engages the ancient world the Bible was written in. Similar to the broader biblical context and its thematic discussion of corporal punishment, we must also read the biblical "rod beating" instructions first of all from the vantage point or horizon of their ancient social context (not ours). Evidence from the ancient world ought to help us adjust our lens in looking at and more clearly understanding the biblical texts about beating children. This ancient-world lens will be an extensive part of our journey within this book (chaps. 3-4). In later chapters we will see that certain ancient law codes, far beyond merely having beatings that left marks and bruises, actually prescribed the physical mutilation of children. Some ANE law codes instruct cutting off a child's hand or tongue, or plucking out a child's eyes as part of the corporal discipline package. Given this sort of ancient-world context, it is extremely hard, if not impossible, to come to any other conclusion about the Bible than a distasteful one that I do not wish to hold. I might state the conclusion this way: *Within its concrete-specific level of instruction the Bible teaches the virtue of marks and bruises for all recipients of corporal punishment, children included.* I shudder at this conclusion. I don't like the idea of beatings with the rod that leave marks or bruises on either adults or children. But I cannot escape it.

Do I still think that the teaching of "no marks or bruises" by contemporary Christian pro-spankers is good? Yes, absolutely! I think that their going beyond the concrete instructions of the Bible in the development of a more realized biblical ethic for today is wonderful. Obviously, we can no longer stay with the concrete-specific instructions about corporal punishment as we read them in a face-value manner on the pages of the Bible. To do so would be unbiblical in some important ways. So our journey has begun.

THE INSTRUMENT OF DISCIPLINE

I have to chuckle at some anti-spanking rhetoric by Christians who think that the "child and rod" proverbs in the Bible do not involve physical beatings at all. This popular notion among many lay Christians connects the "rod" of the child-discipline texts in Proverbs not with an instrument for beating children but with an instrument for shepherding a flock of sheep. As the argument goes, a shepherd does not hit the sheep with his rod but rather guides them gently along on the path that they should take.[35]

---

[35]I first heard this anti-spanking argument when a retired Christian pediatrician (a very godly and gentle man) was lecturing in our church to parents on these Proverbs texts and giving advice on raising children. He taught that the word *rod*, since it was used in Psalm 23 of a

Such shepherding rod interpretations of the discipline texts of Proverbs amount to a lexical fallacy known as illegitimate totality transfer. These anti-spankers wrongly drag material from one context into another just because they share the same word. Furthermore, this shepherd's rod interpretation conveniently forgets that the Hebrew word *beat* or *hit (nakah)* often goes along with the word *rod* in the discipline proverbs—an example of this combination is found in Proverbs 23:13-14. So the hitting or striking function of the rod within the corporal discipline passages is explicit and is different from the shepherding passages.[36]

Pro-spanking scholars rightly argue that the rod is an instrument used in bodily discipline to hit the child. As pictured on the cover of this book, for many years the Christian norm was to use a hickory stick or a switch of some sort. Apparently, the English expression "rule of thumb" was coined to indicate the size limit on the thickness of the stick or switch that the parent used in beating the child. Over time this rod or stick idea morphed into the use of flatter objects (like a paddle or a wide belt) in order to lessen the chance of breaking the skin and bruising. At one point some argued against the use of the hand in discipline (this was popular a generation ago) because the hand might somehow be associated with the parent in a problematic fashion.[37] Others suggest that kids are smart enough to make the connection to the parent whether the instrument of discipline is an object in the hand or the hand itself. They suggest that there is an advantage in using an open hand for a smack on the buttocks because (1) it provides a broad base for diffusion of the blow, and (2) the parent can feel the impact or strength of the blow, which he or she cannot do as easily with a physical

shepherd's staff, should not be understood as an instrument for striking children (how dreadful) but as a metaphor of how we need to gently guide them along the way of life.

[36]The agricultural use of the rod is probably derived from driving stubborn animals in the correct direction. For example, the rod is used to "strike" Balaam's uncooperative donkey (Num 22:22-27). Compare Prov 26:3, where the connection between driving animals and people is fairly obvious: "A whip for the horse, a bridle for the donkey, / and a rod for the back of fools."

[37]Cf. Dobson, *New Dare to Discipline*, p. 64. Dobson thinks the hand might be problematic because of possible connections with the parent and confusion with positive occasions of physical touch. But he also says that the issue is not critical to him and advises parents (who think otherwise) to do what they feel is right (i.e., use a switch, a paddle or the hand).

object. Thus the intent of choosing an alternative instrument other than the rod is tied to the related issue of not leaving marks or bruising—whether one chooses a flat object or giving a smack with an open palm. If we think in terms of introductory physics, the palm (or flat object) diffuses the distribution of impact over a greater number of square inches. Physical damage is far less likely.

Regardless of what you favor personally regarding the instrument of discipline (or even if you endorse a metaphorical rod and advocate only noncorporal discipline), I hope you can see what is happening in contemporary Christian application. We might think that dropping the "rod of discipline" is trivial. But once again the change represents real and significant ethical development and not a mere exchange of cultural equivalents. Swapping the rod for an alternative instrument carries ethical or moral weight given the reasoning behind it. For many people the movement away from the rod (and the "rule of thumb" setting the size limit) is based in concerns over not wanting to leave marks and the degree to which a narrow, curved surface can easily bring greater physical damage than a broad, flat one. If the previous issue, going beyond the Bible discussion about marks and bruises, is a moral issue (indicating abuse), then the choice of instrument cannot be brushed off as a mere swapping of equivalents. Thus the contemporary move by Christians away from the rod, like today's pro-spanking stance of "no marks allowed," indicates an attempt to find higher moral ground. It is not a neutral move; it is a good thing.

FREQUENCY AND OFFENSES PUNISHABLE

Evangelical scholars advocating corporal punishment for children today generally restrict the use of spanking as a "last resort" among multiple disciplinary options and "only for more severe offenses" of a "willfully defiant" nature; thus spanking ought to be "relatively infrequent" compared with other disciplinary measures and especially so as children get older.[38] These four restrictions—last resort, sever-

---

[38]On "last resort" Wegner states, "this level of discipline [corporal punishment] should only be used when previous levels have not curbed the child's misbehavior" ("Discipline in the Book of

est offenses, willful defiance and infrequent usage—provide an operational framework that governs the contemporary Christian spanking scene.

However, do these restrictions align well with the Bible? No, not really. Not if we are trying to align our lives with the concrete specificity of the Bible's teachings. Let's look first at frequency. Once again, the ancient Jewish perspective found in the Wisdom of Sirach may well be closer to that of the Hebrew Bible than our contemporary conjectures. If so, we might want to listen to its call for the frequent beating of children: "He who loves his son will whip him *often* [frequently]" (Sir 30:1). In Sirach it is also said that certain slaves are so much in need of frequent beatings that they will never lack for bruising marks (Sir 23:10). Along similar lines Proverbs encourage parents not to withhold the rod but to be diligent in its application (Prov 13:24). Our old English adage "spare the rod, spoil the child" captures well the biblical sense of urgency and possibly even a sense of frequency—whenever it is needed! If we are committed today to a concrete-specific biblical framing of disciplinary ethic, then frequency ought not to be determined by artificial restrictions imported from our foreign context. Rather, frequency should be set simply by the need for corrective behavior. Sometimes this means lots; sometimes it means only a little.

Furthermore, the issue of frequency is closely connected to the range and type of offenses that were punished with the rod or whip. Unlike modern spankers who want to restrict corporal punishment to willful defiance (severe offenses), the biblical parameters for its usage are much broader. Within the maximum limit of forty stripes, Deuteronomy 25:2

Proverbs," pp. 724-25). Cf. the same "last resort" point within Wegner's citation of The Family Research Council guidelines 2-3 (ibid., p. 731). Dobson's well-known expression "willful defiance" has become the classic articulation for the type of child behavior that warrants spanking (Dobson, *New Dare to Discipline*, p. 61; ibid., *New Strong-Willed Child*, p. 100). Focus on the Family similarly holds that "a child should not be punished for behavior that is not willfully defiant" and places a heavy emphasis on alternative noncorporal means of discipline first and exclusively in the case of school-age children. See Focus on the Family, "Can You Provide Me with Some General Principles and Guidelines for Disciplining My Elementary School Child?" On the frequency of discipline, see Köstenberger, *God, Marriage and Family*, p. 161; Wegner, "Discipline in the Book of Proverbs," pp. 731-32, points 3 and 6.

talks about the number of lashes being "proportionate to the offense."
Due to the generic nature of this Deuteronomy text (no specific crime
in view) the rod and whip were understood within Israel as the broadest
means of punishment and thus used for a wide range of offenses. Some
have estimated that over 160 offenses would have received corporal
punishment.[39] This very broad range of offenses helps us understand
Jesus' parable about "a light beating" for the slave who did not know
what he was doing versus "a severe beating" for the one who knew what
his master wanted (Lk 12:47-48). The contemporary restriction of
spanking to only willful or high-handed defiance (not for lesser offenses) simply does not square with the biblical evidence.

EMOTIVE DISPOSITION OF THE PARENT

Finally, advocates of spanking have developed very clear teaching
about the emotive disposition of the parent administering physical
discipline: "Spank in love, not anger." Along these lines Wegner
writes, "Wise parents always discipline *in love, never in anger,* with
the purpose of helping the child."[40] Along similar lines, Al Mohler
speaks decisively about "never using spanking as a *demonstration of
anger or wrath.*"[41] As a part of various biblical principles guiding the
topic, Köstenberger likewise argues that physical discipline ought to
be administered "in *love* and *not anger.*"[42] Speaking on behalf of Focus
on the Family, Walt Larimore defends a parent's right to physical

---

[39]R. G. Van Yelyr, *The Whip and Rod: An Account of Corporal Punishment Among All Nations and for All Purposes* (London: G. G. Swan, 1948), pp. 10-11. I do not know how accurate this 160-plus figure is. However, it seems reasonable given the breadth of crimes for which the punishment of the whip was applied. Most scholars concur that flogging was one of the broad-est forms of punishment for violating the Torah. For an introductory discussion see Haim H. Cohen, "Flogging," in *Encyclopedia Judaica* (Jerusalem: Keter, 1972), 6:1348-51.

[40]Wegner, "Discipline in the Book of Proverbs," p. 728, italics added; cf., p. 725.

[41]Albert Mohler, "Should Spanking Be Banned? Parental Authority Under Assault," Cross-walk.com, published June 22, 2004, <www.crosswalk.com/1269621>, italics added.

[42]Köstenberger, *God, Marriage and Family*, p. 161. Cf. Wegner, "Discipline in the Book of Prov-erbs," p. 724 n. 47. Köstenberger cites Eph 6:4 and Col 3:21 as support for this "in love not anger" approach. However, neither of these two Pauline verses really achieves what Kösten-berger wants to say about "no parental anger" in physical discipline. The explicit admonition to "not provoke a child to anger" says nothing about the emotive disposition of the parent ad-ministering physical discipline. There are several assumed logical steps that, if articulated, would probably not hold up under scrutiny in light of a biblical theology about anger and the rod (as will be argued next).

discipline, but with this same emotive restriction, "Parents should *never discipline their children in anger.*"[43] This "love but no anger" approach to the physical discipline of children has become almost a mantra for proponents of spanking.

Frankly, I like the "love but no anger" emotive restriction. It provides a genuinely positive and constructive framework for spanking. Combined perhaps with a cooling off period for the parent, a conscious mental check of one's emotional state and, if possible, the presence of another adult within earshot for accountability, this sort of "love but no anger" approach is a great plank within the platform of today's spanking advocates.[44] Unfortunately, it simply is not a biblical concept (if Christians view their discipline practices as biblical because they are based on the concrete-specific teaching of the Bible's rod texts). Of course, the notion of physical beatings as an expression of parental love is very biblical.[45] But the contemporary banning of parental anger is highly problematic. In fact, the restriction of "no anger" in spanking goes directly against a biblical and theological development of corporal punishment.

Before introducing the anger component, we need to examine parallels between disciplinary actions in heaven and those on earth. A strong correlation exists within the Bible between God disciplining his people and human parents disciplining their children. Here are a few texts where the connection is explicit:

> Know then in your heart that as a parent disciplines a child so the
> LORD your God disciplines you. (Deut 8:5)

> I [Yahweh] will punish their transgression with the rod
> and their iniquity with scourges [from the whip]. (Ps 89:32)

> I [Yahweh] will be a father to him, and he shall be a son to me. When
> he commits iniquity, I will punish him with a rod such as mortals use,
> with blows inflicted by human beings. (2 Sam 7:14)

---

[43]Walt Larimore, quoted in "Focus on the Family Defends Parents' Right to Discipline," Cross walk.com, published July 8, 2002, <www.crosswalk.com/1145078>, italics added.

[44]This "within earshot" adult accountability can be accomplished today far more easily than in the past because of cell phones and other communication technology.

[45]See Prov 3:12; 13:24; Heb 12:6; Rev 3:19; cf. Sir 30:1.

My child, do not despise the LORD's discipline
   or be weary of his reproof,
for the LORD reproves the one he loves,
   as a father the son in whom he delights.
      (Prov 3:11-12; cf. Heb 12:5-7)[46]

Of course, these texts are metaphorical or analogical. They depict how God relates to his covenant people in a way that draws upon well-known disciplinary relationships between a father and his children. Notice that the two typical instruments—the rod and whip—are spoken of within the analogy.

Now the difficulty with a no-anger policy for spanking, if it is indeed based on the Bible, is that when God practices corporal punishment, his use of the rod and whip clearly does involve anger. Numerous texts speak of (1) God disciplining his people in anger, and more specifically of (2) God disciplining his children with the rod or whip as an expression of his anger and wrath. In fact, the emotive connection between anger and the rod of discipline is so direct that the Bible sometimes describes divine corporal punishment with the short-form idiom (3) God's "rod of anger" or "rod of wrath."[47] A selection of these "anger and discipline" or "anger and the rod/whip" examples make the emotive connection fairly clear:

O LORD, do not rebuke me in your anger,
   or discipline me in your wrath. (Ps 6:1; cf. Ps 38:1)[48]

Ah, Assyria, the rod of my anger—
   the club in their hands is my fury! (Is 10:5)

Therefore thus says the Lord GOD of hosts: O my people, who live in Zion, do not be afraid of the Assyrians when they beat you with a rod [i.e., God disciplining his people] and lift up their staff against you as the Egyptians did. For in a very little while my indignation will come

---

[46]See also Job 9:34; 21:9; Is 10:26; 30:32; cf. Jud 8:27; 2 Macc 9:11.

[47]Although God surely practices corporal punishment with parental love, we find no parallel short-form expression "rod of love." Instead, the disciplinary instrument is described as his "rod of anger."

[48]This text does not imply that "disciplining in anger" is wrong. Rather, the psalmist's plea is for mercy beyond the normative or expected. Cf. Jer 10:24. In other words, the expected norm is to receive discipline as an expression of anger for wrong behavior.

to an end, and my anger will be directed to their destruction. (Is 10:24-25).

And the LORD will cause his majestic voice to be heard and the descending blow of his arm to be seen, in furious anger and a flame of devouring fire, with a cloudburst and tempest and hailstones. The Assyrian will be terror-stricken at the voice of the LORD, when he strikes with his rod. (Is 30:30-31; cf. Is 30:27, 32)

I am one who has seen affliction
    under the rod of God's wrath. (Lam 3:1)

So you see the difficulty with statements by biblical scholars admonishing us never to use corporal punishment as an expression of anger or wrath. If it is wrong for human parents to discipline in anger, why do we find anger as an integral part of God's "corporal punishment" patterns?

Having made the case for spanking as an expression of parental anger, would I suggest that pro-spanking scholars and Focus on the Family redraft their no-anger policies? No, not at all. I like the change. We should not assume that the social ethic found in the Bible always portrays an ultimate ethical fulfillment of its redemptive spirit. Chapters two and three will enlarge this redemptive-movement idea. At the level of concrete specificity there is often room for a yet-greater ethical application of Scripture, taking its redemptive spirit further. More importantly, the use of theological analogy does not provide a suitable rational for keeping a particular social convention within our application of the Bible today.[49] For our purposes here, I introduce the theological domain only to suggest the likelihood of parental anger being an understood and accepted part of the human discipline scene for the biblical authors who wrote and lived out those texts within their day.

No explicit anger language is used in the handful of spanking texts within Proverbs. True enough. But that absence is probably due to

---

[49]This difference does not invalidate my seventh point about "lashes/beatings in anger" as likely within the realm of the concrete-specific understanding and acceptance by the biblical authors. Nevertheless, it does provide a good reason to ensure its removal from the parenting context today. A dictum is not enough. See chapter two. The topic of theological analogy receives more development in Webb, *Slaves, Women and Homosexuals*, pp. 185-92, criterion 14.

anger being an obvious and assumed component of human corporal punishment that naturally mirrors the divine "rod of anger." This appears more likely than to assume that anger was purposefully omitted in order to imply, "Anger is okay for divine discipline, but not for human discipline." It seems that the divine anger depicted in (metaphorical) corporal punishment texts functions as an authentic depiction of God but in language that analogically reflected the reader's human experience—a father, a son and a rod.[50] That way people immediately grasped the theological message.

CONCLUSION

I shudder to think how a Christian *could* practice child discipline today based on the corporal punishment instructions of the Bible. In my own hermeneutical journey it eventually dawned on me that I was artificially deriving the validity of my pro-spanking position based on certain concrete-specific instructions within the corporal punishment material. Yet if I was going to use the biblical text in this concrete fashion, then the Bible had a lot more to say about my beloved two-smacks-max position than what I wanted to hear:

1. Do not be duped by age restrictions. Teenagers and elementary-school children need the rod just as much, if not more, than those in early childhood, and beatings *are* effective (not "ineffective" for older

---

[50] 2 Sam 7:14 explicitly states that the theological rod analogy is drawn from the human sphere of father-child discipline with the rod. Thus it seems probable that the "rod of anger" concept in theological discourse comes from that same father-son human discipline setting. For everyday examples of the connection between human beatings with the rod and anger, see Num 22:27; Jer 37:15. For one human example of the "rod of anger" see Prov 22:8, "Whoever sows injustice will reap calamity, / and the rod of anger will fail." The meaning of this proverb and especially the second half—"the rod of anger will fail"—is difficult. Who is wielding the rod and to what end? Perhaps it is the unjust, who are warned that their angry rule will ultimately fail. Such a meaning *may* imply that the "rod of anger" for just or righteous people (unlike the use of the rod with the wicked) will not fail. Accordingly, the verse may provide some, albeit tenuous, evidence of human "beatings expressing anger" as a counterpart to the divine idiom. The fact that this proverb talks about actions of evil or about unjust persons does not remove the possibility that the referential context, even if figuratively used, is that of physical beatings with a disciplinary rod (contra Paul E. Koptak, *Proverbs*, NIVAC [Grand Rapids: Zondervan, 2003], p. 519 n. 8). Surely from a biblical perspective there are *just* beatings as well as *unjust* beatings, and these two contexts would involve righteous anger and unrighteous anger in the use of the rod.

children as presently claimed).

2. Forget the idea of a two-smacks-max limit. Apply a gradual increase in the number of strokes so that it fuses better with the forty strokes cap for adults.

3. Get the location right. Lashes are made for the "backs of fools" not for their bottoms.

4. Remove the "no bruising" restriction. Bruises, welts and wounds should be viewed as a virtue—the evidence of a sound beating.

5. Pick the right instrument. A good rod (hickory stick) will inflict far more intense pain and bruising than a hand on the bottom.

6. Stop thinking about corporal punishment as a last resort. Use the rod for nonvolitional misdemeanors as well as for major infractions.

7. Drop the notion of "love but no anger." Mix in a little righteous anger with your use of the rod.

The contents of this chapter should cause Christians to rethink what we mean by our parenting and discipline practices being "biblical." A truly biblical Christianity should not appeal to the Bible and its concrete-specific instructions about "beatings with the rod" in order to validate the morality of spanking children in our contemporary world.

As we ponder this first chapter, it should become clear to all readers how much of the present-day two-smacks-max spanking ethic and its seven ways of going beyond the Bible (beyond its concrete-specific instructions) is moving with gradual, incremental steps toward something better in the treatment of children. This insight provides a powerful hermeneutical awakening for our lives.

On what basis, then, can today's two-smacks-max spanking proponents argue that their sevenfold journey beyond the Bible's teaching on corporal punishment is in fact *biblical*? That is the task of our next two chapters—the slavery texts (chap. 2) and the rod and whip texts (chap. 3). With chapter two we temporarily leave the corporal punishment texts and look at the slavery texts in order to explore hermeneutical method by utilizing an example from the Christian past. That slavery chapter allows us to become familiar with a redemptive-movement hermeneutic and understand its approach in a more neutral context before returning to the debated issue of this book. With chapter three I use the redemptive-movement model in order to think about the rod and whip texts from an entirely different vantage point than this opening chapter. I will ask how we can legitimately abandon or move beyond many aspects of the corporal punishment texts, while at the same time remaining true to the Bible. In both of these next two chapters a redemptive-movement approach to Scripture offers comfort to the Christian soul (without overlooking troublesome corporal punishment texts within the Bible) and provides an approach to Scripture that resolves the hermeneutical inconsistencies outlined in this first chapter.

PART II

A Redemptive-Movement Hermeneutic

2

THE SLAVERY TEXTS

A REDEMPTIVE-MOVEMENT MODEL

Chapters three and four provide a solution to the ethical dilemmas and hermeneutical inconsistencies raised in the first section of this book. To put it another way, the next two chapters help ease my troubled soul as a Christian struggling with difficult texts in the Bible. These chapters suggest that we should understand the rod and whip texts through a redemptive-movement model. Yet it might be helpful to learn the approach first within slavery texts where the church has already come to an antislavery or abolitionist consensus in its ethical conclusions. Accordingly, this chapter (chap. 2) will acquaint readers with the redemptive-movement model through a discussion of the slavery texts. Then, in chapter three a redemptive-movement approach will be used to understand and apply the corporal punishment texts.

The present chapter unfolds in three parts. I will first present an overview of a redemptive-movement hermeneutic (along with a pictorial sketch) to give a bird's-eye view of how the method works. Second, the bulk of the chapter will look at the slavery texts of Scripture in order to illustrate a redemptive-movement approach. Third, I will show how a redemptive-movement approach fits within a grammatical-historical method and, in fact, helps us do a better job of classic grammatical-historical exegesis and application.

The point of this chapter is to give the reader a background understanding of a redemptive-movement hermeneutic before engaging the rod and whip texts in the Bible. Please do not skip over this crucial material. Readers will understand chapter three much better if they have first wrestled with the hermeneutical concepts discussed in this slavery chapter.

A REDEMPTIVE-MOVEMENT APPROACH: AN OVERVIEW

In broad terms Christians often tend toward one of two ways of approaching the Bible: (1) with a *redemptive-movement* appropriation of Scripture, which at times encourages movement beyond its concrete-specific instructions in order to pursue an ultimate application of Scripture that yields a greater fulfillment of its redemptive spirit, or (2) with a more *static* or *stationary* appropriation of Scripture that locks itself into the concrete specificity of, or as close as possible to, exactly what is found on the page in somewhat of a face-value manner. The latter generally understands the words of the text in isolation from their cultural, historical and canonical contexts, and with minimal—or no—emphasis on their underlying spirit, thus restricting contemporary application to how the words of the text were applied in their original setting. But to do so often leads to a *mis*appropriation of the text precisely because the interpreter has failed to extend further or reapply the redemptive spirit of the original text in a later cultural setting. As will be argued, it is a trajectory or logical extension of the Bible's redemptive spirit or redemptive trend that carries Christians toward an ultimate ethical application of Scripture.[1]

In figure 2.1, notice the strikingly different facial expressions of the person reading the Bible. It is the same person but looking at the Bible from two different perspectives or horizons. When people view the Bible from the *left side* of the diagram, they read Scripture through the lens of its ancient-world context, namely, the ancient Near East (ANE) for the Old Testament or the Greco-Roman setting and second-temple Judaism for the New Testament. Now let's change horizons. When people operate from the *right side* of the diagram, they are reading the Bible through the lens of their contemporary

---

[1]This overview section has been adapted from William J. Webb, *Slaves, Women and Homosexuals* (Downers Grove, Ill.: IVP Academic, 2001).

culture and especially (for purposes of this diagram) in a particular situation where our present-day ethic in select cases happens to have advanced in some degree beyond the static form of the biblical text toward something better. Often the right-side reading leaves Christians with a disturbing question mark in their minds about issues of applicability or even relevance of a biblical ethic for our contemporary world. As in chapter one, there are at least seven unsettling ways in which biblical instructions about the rod and whip texts are indeed troublesome. Even without a hermeneutical framework for doing so, pro-spankers have instinctively gone beyond the concrete-specific teaching of the Bible in their two-smacks-max approach with incremental steps toward a better ethic—a better realization of a *biblical* ethic, as we will see. From the right-side vantage point the Bible looks repressive or regressive. But enough said about the corporal punishment texts. We will return to that topic in chapter three.

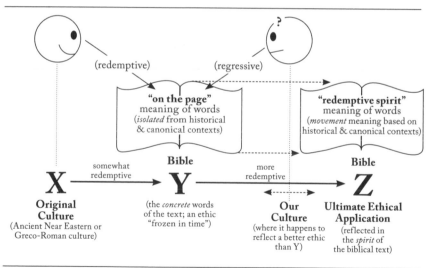

Figure 2.1. Two hermeneutical perspectives

You can understand why the person on the right looks perplexed or disturbed. Let's explore this "question mark" response through a completely different example. For instance, imagine a contemporary Christian in our Western context reading Deuteronomy 21:10-14. I will cite the passage in full:

When you go to war against your enemies and the LORD your God de-
livers them into your hands and you take captives, if you notice among
the captives a beautiful woman and are attracted to her, you may take
her as your wife. Bring her into your home and have her shave her head,
trim her nails and put aside the clothes she was wearing when captured.
After she has lived in your house and mourned her father and mother
for a full month, then you may go to her and be her husband and she
shall be your wife. If you are not pleased with her, let her go wherever
she wishes. You must not sell her or treat her as a slave, since you have
dishonored her. (NIV)[2]

We might say that this war text is "exposure challenged" in Christianity today and that it has in effect been banned from public readings
in our contemporary churches. The reason should be obvious. As
Christians read this text, it begins to dawn on them that the Bible contains a war ethic that includes "grabbing hot-looking women" as wives.
This should rightly be a disturbing feature within the text as we read
our Bibles today. It is unlikely that Christians will mount a lobby group
that attempts to bring this text into legislation through Congress or
Parliament as a way in which we ought to treat female prisoners in our
modern war context, nor for that matter is it the way we want our enemies to treat their prisoners (us) today.

So what happens as Christians today read a text like Deuteronomy
21:10-14? Well, most contemporary readers of the biblical war texts
(often unknowingly) read these texts through the lens of the Geneva or
Hague war conventions. Our everyday, street-level discussions about
the treatment of war captives are very much governed by these documents. Whether people are aware of it or not, even media coverage
about the ethics of taking pictures of war captives is dominated by these
modern treatises on war ethics. I call them *emerging* treatises for two
reasons. First, there has been a long history of development in military
ethics, a summary of which is easily accessible on the Web.[3] Second, I
do not want to give the impression that even these latest war conven-

---

[2]Cf. Num 31:25-32; Deut 20:14.
[3]For the Geneva War Convention and other treaties governing our conduct of war see "The
Avalon Project: The Laws of War," <http://avalon.law.yale.edu/subject_menus/lawwar.asp>.

tions, as good as they are, have somehow reached an ultimate war, or violent-force, ethical application of the redemptive spirit within Scripture (fig. 2.1 position Z = ultimate ethical application).

But let's come back to the left side of the diagram (position X). Sometimes I talk with Christians and non-Christians alike who are extremely disturbed when they encounter the "grabbing hot-looking women" war text of Deuteronomy 21. While not abandoning a right-side reflection on the text through the lens of the Geneva and Hague war conventions, I encourage them to begin by reading Scripture from an entirely different vantage point, namely, the ANE contexts within which they originally emerged.[4] If we are to understand these biblical texts, we need to be reading ancient extrabiblical war documents from Egypt, Assyria, Babylonia and so forth. Once people do this, they discover that the ancient treatment of women in war was utterly horrendous—it often included bodily mutilation of women (cutting off their breasts and displaying them on poles), torturous deaths, multiple rapes and a type of concubine enslavement where women would be required to perform perpetual sexual favors or produce offspring for their owners.[5] In ancient siege warfare the fate of female captives was considered so dreadful that, if it looked like a city was about to fall, the men at times killed their own wives. What an utterly ugly world—the mistreatment of humans by other humans is sometimes staggering. In our present-day context this ancient war portrait shares some commonality with the rape camps of Rwanda.

Placing the biblical text within that sort of ancient-world war context allows us to see Deuteronomy 21:10-14 in a different light. Israelite warriors were not permitted to rape or mutilate a woman captive; they had to wait at least a month as a minimum delay—a cooling off period—before any sexual contact.[6] Furthermore, in order to have sexual

---

[4]*ANE* provides a summary way of speaking about the various neighboring countries and the larger ancient-world setting where Israel was "planted" and lived out its faith in Yahweh. When Scripture is read in light of that ancient-world horizon (and not ours), it provides the best vantage point from which to sense its redemptive spirit because it gives us clues about how God was acting in some sort of redemptive fashion.

[5]See William J. Webb, *Brutal, Bloody and Barbaric: War Texts That Trouble the Soul* (Downers Grove, Ill.: InterVarsity, forthcoming).

[6]While the shaved head permitted at least some expression of ancient mourning, it also made

intercourse with a captive woman, the captor had to marry her. Should the marriage not work out, the woman went free; she could not be held or sold as a slave. By reading the biblical text within its ancient context, we begin to hear its redemptive movement. Now it is the further development or greater fulfillment of this core redemptive trend—the better treatment of female prisoners in war—that ought to carry Christians forward in forging new documents that help offset or minimize the atrocities of war. The implications of the redemptive movement within the text, which I alternatively call its "redemptive spirit," ought to inspire Christians to venture into contemporary war discussions with the intention, wherever possible, of even "going beyond" the Geneva and Hague conventions. We do not want to stay with the static or frozen-in-time ethic reflected in the concrete-specific instructions of the Bible; rather Christians need to embrace the redemptive spirit of the text and journey toward an ultimate ethical application of that spirit.

In sum, the essence of a redemptive-movement model can be captured succinctly in three or four words: Movement is (crucial) meaning. To be sure, movement is not the only meaning within the text. But movement provides absolutely crucial meaning that is often lost by contemporary readers as we wrestle with how to apply the text in today's setting. We might alternatively depict an "on the page" or static type of meaning as one derived by reading the words of a text *only* within its immediate literary context—up and down the page. This literary context for discerning meaning is also important. But it is movement meaning captured from reading a text in (1) its ancient *historical and social* context, and (2) its *canonical* context, which yields a sense of the underlying spirit of the biblical text. (Canonical movement will be illustrated in the following slavery discussion.) It is this redemptive-movement or redemptive-spirit meaning that ought to radically shape the contours of our contemporary ethical portrait.

THE SLAVERY TEXTS
Suppose we explore the concept of meaning derived from redemptive

---

the physical beauty of the female captive less obvious. Aside from the waiting period, this reduced physical attraction would also help with a cooling-off function.

movement—"movement meaning"—through the lens of several slavery texts. We could begin with that seldom-preached text of Exodus 21:20-21, "If a man beats his male or female slave with a rod and the slave dies as a direct result, he must be punished, but he is not to be punished if the slave gets up after a day or two, since the slave is his property" (NIV). We might paraphrase it as follows: "A Hebrew slave owner must not kill or severely incapacitate slaves when beating them (such would bring an undefined penalty), but otherwise the slave owner is legally free to beat the 'living day lights' out of a slave, provided the slave is able to get up after a day or two."[7] This text ought to disturb contemporary Christians, for it enshrines the right of slave masters to beat their slaves, it permits a latitude of punishment that could well have included very bloody and brutal beatings, and it does so by positively invoking (instead of rejecting) the notion of people as property. Such "on the page" meaning of this text can be easily detected from its immediate lexical, grammatical and literary context.

This slave-beating text is at times cited by those opposed to the Christian faith. Although I have never heard this beating text preached from a church pulpit, I have heard it cited by several non-Christians— by my neighbors at a New Year's Eve party, by students on a university campus after I had given a lecture on social ethics, and by secular ethicists who want to dispose of the Bible altogether as a basis for contemporary ethics. They often ask a similar question, "You believe in a God who would say it is okay [no judicial recrimination] to beat slaves within a hair's breadth of their life, provided they walk after a day or two? That's the God you believe in? That's the Bible you follow?"

When responding, I genuinely empathize with their position. I spend a good deal of time talking in detail about the way a text such as this troubles my soul. But eventually I get around to making the point that I do not think they (my non-Christian opponents) have read the text correctly. On one such occasion a person actually grabbed a nearby

---

[7]There is nothing within the New Testament that would automatically or directly rescind the biblical authority and ease-of-applicability of this Old Testament instruction (Ex 21:20-21) if a New Testament slave owner were looking for explicit advice from God about how to interact with disobedient slaves.

Bible and read it to me just to show me that he had indeed cited the Bible correctly. There it is, right on the page! After a deliberate and lengthy pause, I responded again, "No, I still think that you have not read that text correctly."

When given an opportunity to explain, I talk about how we need to read the slave-beating text of Exodus 21 within its ancient historical and social context in order to capture its movement meaning. What I argue is this: If we are going to read the biblical text with all of its intended meaning and not lose important components of that meaning, then we must read the text within the ancient-world context and its canonical context. For example, in the ANE setting there was nothing holding back masters from beating a slave to death if they wished.[8] The only consideration that curtailed such a brutal act was the loss of the slave's productivity. Yet such a utilitarian value often gave way to making a point to the larger slave community. Beating a slave to death was not an unheard of practice, and some masters exercised such rights in order to send a clear message to the rest of their slaves. It was a cruel method of social control for the larger slave community. When you read Exodus 21:20-21 in that sort of ancient social context, you have to say, "Okay, I see some movement. I see distinct redemptive movement away from the surrounding cultural context and toward something better."[9]

To this slave-beating portrait we must add other texts within the Bible (Ex 21:26-27) that say, if in beating a slave, the slave is injured physically—he or she loses a tooth, an eye, an ear or the like—then the slave must go free. Once again, a riverlike current of meaning runs far deeper than an isolated understanding of words on the page.

---

[8]For space considerations I will generally not cite ancient sources throughout this discussion of slavery. For a more detailed development of ANE and Greco-Roman sources see Webb, *Slaves, Women and Homosexuals.*

[9]The term for "punished" in Ex 21:20 is literally "avenged," which in the sense of the Old Testament blood-avenger concept might mean that the slave owner was to be put to death (see James K. Bruckner, *Exodus,* NIBC [Peabody, Mass.: Hendrickson, 2008], p. 204). If this interpretation is correct, then the degree of redemptive movement for the Ex 21:20-21 text relative to the ANE environment would be even greater than what I have proposed here. The evidence is intriguing but not conclusive because the term can have nontechnical usages that do not necessarily infer a direct one-for-one blood avenging.

We must read these slave-beating texts within their ancient context where masters (both ANE and Greco-Roman) often in punishing slaves intentionally left physical mutilations in all kinds of horrendous ways in order to make a lasting visual statement to the rest of the slave community and to give the disobedient slave a perpetual reminder that something similar or worse might happen in the future. Within this harsh ancient-world setting we again recognize a wonderful aspect of movement. Yes, the Bible allows beatings, but if any physical mutilation occurred, that mutilation meant the slave went free! The impact of hearing the redemptive-movement of the Bible as read within its broader ANE context can often be captured in one English word, *Wow!* These Old Testament texts do not only regulate social behavior, they do much more. They provide a crucial element of movement that captures and conveys the Bible's redemptive spirit—the integral heartbeat of the text as it incrementally moves people toward an ultimate ethical application of the Bible (point Z in fig. 2.1).

We could go on with the text of Deuteronomy 23:15-16 (cf. Is 16:3-4), which provides safety and refuge to slaves that run away from foreign countries and forbids returning them to their country of origin. Just reading the isolated words of this text sounds rather hohum and blah, especially for contemporary Western readers who automatically listen to the biblical text with abolitionist assumptions. But understanding it within an ancient-world setting yields for us the extent of its movement and clearly reveals a redemptive trend that is emerging within the Bible. In the ancient world runaway slaves were sought for bounty. Captured slaves were at times executed in a brutal and torturous fashion, along with their families and accomplices. The ancient Code of Hammurabi prescribed the death penalty for even aiding a runaway slave. Most nations held extradition treaties for the return of slaves. In a radical departure from these prevalent views, Israel became a safety zone and functioned like a country of refuge for foreign runaway slaves. Now I read the Bible within this ancient-world environment and once again I have to say, "Ah, redemptive-movement meaning!" That is my God. He *is* concerned about social ethics beyond simply regulating society and maintaining its current standards. He is concerned to move a much-entrenched social institution with incremental steps toward a better treatment of human beings.

To this slavery portrait we must add the powerful components of canonical development, especially as we read texts like Galatians 3:28 and Colossians 3:11 where the "neither slave nor free" statements forge a new understanding of how members relate to each other within the body of Christ. As these verses are read against the backdrop of the Old Testament, second temple Judaism and Greco-Roman culture, at least on a theoretical level, there is an awakening to a new kind of social equality within the church. The radical concept of equality in the new "in Christ" society, like the underlying ideology that transformed Jew and Gentile relationships in the first century, was eventually heard by the church with a more fully developed outworking of its yet unrealized or only partially realized ethic. So it is the movement meaning within the slavery texts themselves that serves to connect the biblical text to an *ultimate ethical application*, namely, an abolitionist ethic. To put it another way, the objective of a redemptive-movement hermeneutic is to move toward a fuller realization of the redemptive spirit or the redemptive trend already begun within Scripture.

Consequently, the slavery texts ought to be understood from two distinctly different perspectives or horizons. Both of them are legitimate. On the one hand, there is a difficult or painful side to the portrait. As we read the biblical texts about slaves, an overwhelming impression emerges: *a less-than-ultimate ethic in the treatment of slaves/ people is a major part of our Bible's concrete specificity*. If we clear away the technical language, we might simply say that there is a problem with the treatment of slaves in the Bible. There exist numerous not-so-pretty components within the slavery texts that illustrate a less-than-ultimate ethic in the treatment of slaves/people:

- Human beings/slaves are considered to be property (Ex 12:44; 21:20-21, 32; Lev 22:11).

- Foreign slaves in Israel did not experience the seventh year of release (Lev 25:39-46).

- Slaves within Israel were used to produce offspring for their infertile owners (Gen 16:1-4; 30:3-4, 9-10; cf. Gen 35:22).

- Sexual violation of a betrothed slave woman led not to death as in the case of a free woman (Deut 22:25-27) but to a mere payment or offering for damages (Lev 19:20-22).

- A bull owner's liability for the animal's goring a slave to death (compared to a free person) shows tremendous inequality in the valuing of human life (Ex 21:28-32).

- Slave owners were permitted to beat their slaves without any penalty, provided the slave survived and could get up after a couple of days (Ex 21:20-21).

But to call this treatment of slaves "abusive" in terms of the original culture would be anachronistic. Relative to the ancient culture many of these texts were in some measure progressive. Nevertheless, the practices listed here are problematic and in need of movement toward an ultimate ethical application of the redemptive trend that Scripture has already initiated. A much more humane treatment of persons can be legislated and lived out in our modern civil-law settings. The idea of a redemptive-movement hermeneutic is not that God himself has somehow "moved" in his thinking or that Scripture is in any way less than God's Word. Rather, it means that God in a pastoral sense accommodates himself to meeting people and society where they are in their existing social ethic and (from there) he gently moves them with incremental steps toward something better. Moving large, complex and embedded social structures along an ethical continuum is by no means a simple matter. Incremental movement within Scripture reveals a God who is willing to live with the tension between an absolute ethic in theory and the reality of guiding real people in practice toward such a goal.

Fortunately, there exists a wonderful and inspiring side to the biblical portrait of slaves. It is this positive side that establishes *redemptive movement as crucial meaning within the biblical text.* This meaning derived from observing movement and thus the text's redemptive spirit must profoundly shape the course of our contemporary appropriation of the Bible in a way that often carries us beyond the bound-in-time components of meaning within the biblical text. In the next set of examples the hermeneutical task is to "listen to" and "hear" the slavery texts within their cultural-historical context (relative to the ancient world) and their canonical context (with movement to the New Testament). In both cases, by hearing biblical texts in this manner, we begin to sense a wonderful redemptive trend as part of the biblical words about slavery:

- Holidays granted to slaves for festivals and for the weekly sabbath rest, compared with the ancient world, were generous (Deut 16:10-12; Ex 23:12).

- In both Testaments slaves are included in the worship setting (Ex 12:44; Deut 12:12, 18; cf. Col 3:22-25; 4:16) and the New Testament church community profoundly raised a slave's status yet further to equality "in Christ" (Gal 3:28). Some ancient cultures (such as the Roman Empire) restricted slaves from involvement in the sacred rituals and religious festivals because they were thought to have a defiling or polluting influence.

- No-interest loans within Israel functioned as a preventative measure to reduce the occurrence of debt slavery (Lev 25:35-36; Deut 15:1-2, 7-11); this contrasts with loan rates in the surrounding foreign nations that were often well in excess of 20 percent interest.

- The legislated release of Hebrew debt slaves after a certain number of years, when compared with most of the ancient world, is a highly redemptive aspect of biblical legislation especially as it is framed in terms of human dignity (Lev 25:39-43; cf. Jer 34:8-22).

- Material assistance for released slaves stands out as a generous act of biblical law (Deut 15:12-18).

- Limitations were placed on the severity of physical beatings (Ex 21:20-21), and freedom was granted to any slave who was physically damaged (Ex 21:26-27). Other ancient cultures did not limit the slave owner's power in this way. In fact, torturous abuse of select slaves and intentional maiming and disfigurement often became an object lesson for others.

- Masters are admonished to turn away from harshness and to show genuine care for their slaves (Eph 6:9; Col 4:1), transforming the slave-master relationship with a new sense of Christian brotherhood (Philem 16).

- Scripture denounces foreign countries (Gaza and Tyre) for stealing people in order to trade them as slaves (Ex 21:16; Deut 24:7; cf. 1 Tim 1:10).

- In the ancient world runaway slaves were sought for bounty. Captured slaves were often executed along with their families and accomplices. In a radical departure from these prevalent views, Scripture outlawed any extradition so that Israel became a safety zone and refuge for foreign runaway slaves (Deut 23:15-16; cf. Is 16:3-4).

When the Bible's slavery texts are read against the ANE and Greco-Roman context, redemptive movement becomes increasingly clear. These biblical modifications to the existing social norms brought greater protection and dignity for the slave. This improvement in the conditions of slaves relative to the original culture was clearly a redemptive action on the part of Scripture. Admittedly, it was not redemptive in any absolute sense. To use a football metaphor, Scripture moved the cultural "scrimmage markers" only so far downfield. Yet that movement was sufficient to signal a clear direction and the possibility of further improvements for later generations. Redemptive-movement meaning was (and is) absolutely crucial to our application of Scripture. This meaning within biblical texts—yes, even within the slave-beating texts—should by logical extension of their underlying redemptive spirit take us to an abolitionist ethic. In so doing, an aspect of meaning from words within the slavery texts (not simply from without) becomes the basis for our present-day convictions about the abolition of slavery.

In sum, a sense of the redemptive spirit or the incremental ethic within the slavery texts of the Bible—the meaning derived from understanding its movement—is discovered through reading these texts relative to their ancient historical and social setting. Such ancient-context movement is often augmented by further canonical movement between Testaments. This often-missed aspect of meaning derived from movement is a crucial part of biblical authority for Christians wanting to apply the text today. Ultimately, a logical extension or trajectory of the redemptive-spirit meaning is what carries Christians in a credible fashion from the slavery texts to our contemporary affirmation of an abolitionist ethic.

For an in-depth development of a redemptive-movement approach to the slavery texts and one that provides citation from ANE and Greco-Roman slavery sources (not included in this short essay), the reader may wish to consult a fuller discussion in *Slaves, Women and Homosexuals*.[10] I have also answered frequently asked questions about a redemptive-movement hermeneutic elsewhere, so will only cite those sources here.[11]

GRAMMATICAL-HISTORICAL HERMENEUTICS DONE BETTER

Mark Noll's insightful book *The Civil War as a Theological Crisis* illustrates the key role that hermeneutics played during the 1800s in framing how Christians understood the slavery texts.[12] While both the pro-slavery side and the abolitionists appealed to the Bible to support their opposing opinions about slavery in America, their approaches to understanding Scripture were quite different. The *pro-slavery* group typically read the Bible in a static, face-value fashion and tied their ethic to the concrete-specific instructions of the biblical texts. Since there were no explicit instructions within the Bible to abolish slavery, and Christians

---

[10]Webb, *Slaves, Women and Homosexuals*, pp. 30-55, 73-81, 162-72; William J. Webb, "A Redemptive-Movement Hermeneutic: The Slavery Analogy," in *Discovering Biblical Equality: Complementarity Without Hierarchy*, ed. Gordon D. Fee, Rebecca M. Groothuis and Ronald Pierce (Downers Grove, Ill.: InterVarsity Press, 2004), pp. 382-400.

[11]See William J. Webb, "A Redemptive-Movement Hermeneutic: Encouraging Dialogue among Four Evangelical Views," *Journal of the Evangelical Theological Society* 48, no. 2 (2005): 331-49; William J. Webb, "A Redemptive-Movement Model," in *Four Views on Going Beyond the Bible to Theology*, ed. Gary Meadors (Grand Rapids: Zondervan, 2009), pp. 215-48, and my short response essays which follow each of the other three views.

[12]Mark A. Noll, *The Civil War as a Theological Crisis* (Chapel Hill: University of North Carolina Press, 2006), pp. 1-191.

in the New Testament still practiced slavery, there was no reason for them to do any different. The *anti-slavery* side (abolitionists) appealed to the underlying principle and redemptive spirit of Scripture, which grounded their understanding of biblical authority in a more abstracted element of textual meaning and gave them freedom to engage in more rigorous theological reflection about certain unseemly components and the partially (but not fully) realized ethic found in the slavery texts. They argued that abolitionism meant greater dignity and better treatment of human beings.

One thing should be certain from the slavery debates of the past—*a redemptive-movement hermeneutic is not a new hermeneutic.* The appeal to the underlying redemptive spirit of Scripture and intentional movement beyond the concrete specificity of the Bible is precisely what Christians in the 1800s had to do in order to make a case for the abolition of slavery. Anti-slavery proponents realized that it was possible to achieve a greater fulfillment of the biblical ethic (contained in its redemptive spirit) than what was conveyed within the concrete instructions of the slavery texts. In the last two centuries with the discovery of many more ANE and Greco-Roman sources, we have been able to strengthen aspects of their method. As we learn to read Scripture within its ancient-world context, we have been able to join with earlier abolitionist Christians in their journey toward an ultimate ethical application of Scripture. The passion for living out the redemptive spirit of Scripture is the same.

Furthermore, it is important to understand that a redemptive-movement method is not a stand alone hermeneutic. Rather, a redemptive-movement approach fits as *a component within a standard grammatical-historical hermeneutic and application process.* Over the years Christians have worked hard at the *grammatical* side of the hermeneutical equation. Seminaries often train pastors in Greek and Hebrew studies and especially in how to read biblical texts within their grammatical and literary context—up and down the page. This meaning is essential to a good understanding of the Bible. We would be severely impoverished if we did not do this sort of rigorous study of the biblical text. However, Christian scholars and pastors need to devote just as much energy to reading texts within their ancient historical contexts—the *historical* side of the grammatical-historical method. This part of biblical studies has lagged behind in part because it is only now—in more recent days—that vast libraries of ancient literary and nonliterary (historical) sources have become available in order to do the task.

Hopefully this chapter on the slavery texts has renewed a sense of wonder and delight in terms of what God is doing redemptively in Scripture—even in certain texts that at one level are down-right disturbing. The slavery texts, when read within their ancient-world setting, offers good evidence—a kind of proof within the pudding—that using a redemptive-movement approach as a component within a grammatical-historical hermeneutic is far better than not doing so. In short, a redemptive-movement approach is nothing other than *grammatical-historical hermeneutics done better.*

CONCLUSION

I have purposely not jumped headfirst into the corporal punishment texts. Instead, this chapter has presented a redemptive-movement model based on observations from the slavery texts of Scripture. Only by moving beyond the concrete specificity of these biblical texts and by engaging their incremental ethic do we then honor the authorial heartbeat of the biblical text itself. In using a redemptive-movement approach Christians must journey far beyond any surface-level appropriation of Scripture to an application of the text that listens intently to its movement meaning as derived from hearing it within its historical and canonical contexts. When the slavery and corporal punishment texts (as we will see in chap. 3) are read within such ancient contexts, one indeed discovers a profound sense of redemptive-movement meaning. Our task as Christians is not to stay with a static understanding of Scripture but to champion its redemptive spirit in new and fresh ways that logically and theologically extend its movement meaning into today's context.

Now that the redemptive-movement model has been introduced, even newcomers to the method will have acquired enough of an understanding to begin using the approach in the corporal punishment texts of the Bible. This engaging—and I think most exciting—core feature of this book occurs in chapter three, on the rod and the whip. But the use of a redemptive-movement model does not end there. You will also see a redemptive-movement hermeneutic in action again in the essay on the heavy knife (chap. 4) where we wrestle with the hand-amputation text of Deuteronomy 25 and with questions about corporal punishment for adults today.

3

THE ROD AND WHIP TEXTS

A BIBLICAL BASIS FOR GOING BEYOND

In view of the "seven ways" discussion (chap. 1), some Christians might be unhappy that these pro-spankers have gone beyond the concrete instructions of the Bible in forging their discipline practices. Some might be inclined to criticize these spanking advocates for getting their hands caught in the "going beyond" cookie jar. While they champion child-discipline methods that are purportedly based on the biblical text, their approach to corporal punishment goes well beyond the concrete specificity of biblical teaching on the subject. They have departed from the Bible in seven significant ways.

Rather than chastising these pro-spankers for their two-smacks-max spanking ethic, however, this chapter seeks to celebrate and affirm their efforts. It shows that they have gone beyond the Bible *biblically*. By this I mean that their ethical and applicational development rests firmly on a biblical basis. They have forged a contemporary ethic in the area of corporal punishment that takes the redemptive spirit of Scripture to a much better realization of that spirit. They have taken the incremental and unrealized ethic of Scripture to a greater fulfillment of the redemptive trajectory or redemptive trend already begun in Scripture itself. Christians should celebrate this kind of accomplishment. Admittedly, we might still question whether they have gone far enough (a topic for a later chapter), but from my perspective the fact that they have moved at all, and as far as they have, is great. They have made improvements within the contemporary spanking scene that leave the rugged specificity and face-value teaching of the Bible far behind.

Accordingly, this chapter seeks to accomplish two very positive things. First, we will briefly review some of the reasons for the two-smacks-max changes. Rehearsing the reasons for their changes demonstrates that they are quite reasonable and logical; there are good reasons without even engaging the Bible for justification. These extrabiblical reasons for their changes establish that we are talking about significant ethical development and not simply a swapping of ancient and contemporary equivalents. Second, this chapter develops something that is missing in the two-smacks-max pro-spanking position, namely, a biblical basis for their departure from the concrete-specific instructions of Scripture. Here we will utilize a redemptive-movement hermeneutic that embraces their applicational change and celebrates a development in ethic that carries the redemptive spirit of the Bible further. We have seen this hermeneutic already within the slavery texts (chap. 2); now we will see it in the corporal punishment texts.

REASONS FOR THE TWO-SMACKS-MAX CHANGES

There are good reasons for the changes initiated by two-smacks-max pro-spankers today that clearly depart from specific aspects of biblical teaching. Before examining the rationale for their changes, let's review the seven changes (see table 3.1; CP = corporal punishment).

If we recall the rationale for the "going beyond" changes that contemporary pro-spankers have made, we might reflect on the change from beatings on the *back* (Bible) to spankings on the *bottom* (today's two-smacks-max pro-spankers). The reason for the buttocks location as stated by Focus on the Family and by Paul Wegner (citing The Family Research Council) is that this physical location, the buttocks, makes permanent damage very unlikely.[1] Similarly, the movement

---

[1]Paul D. Wegner, "Discipline in the Book of Proverbs: 'To Spank or Not to Spank,'" *Journal of the Evangelical Theological Society* 48 no. 4 (2005): 732; James Dobson, *The New Dare to Discipline*, 2nd ed. (Carol Stream, Ill.: Tyndale House, 1992), p. 63. Cf. the continued emphasis on spanking the buttocks within the post-Dobson Focus organization: Focus on the Family, "Does Spanking Cause Kids to Become Violent?" published April 14, 2010, <http://family.custhelp.com/app/answers/detail/a_id/25648>.

Table 3.1. Seven Changes in Corporal Punishment Views

	Concrete-specific teaching of the Bible	Two-smacks-max spanking ethic
1. Age limitations	no age limits; CP used throughout teen years	primarily preschool age, less so up to age 10-12; no spanking teens
2. Number of lashes	graduated increase to 40 max strokes (reasonable inference within Scripture)	1 or 2 smacks max
3. Bodily location	back	buttocks
4. Bruising, welts and wounds	an acceptable practice; viewed as a virtue	unacceptable practice; viewed as abusive
5. Instrument	rod (or whip)	open palm (broader distribution of impact is less harmful)
6. Frequency and type of offenses	broadly/frequently used; defiant and nondefiant actions	infrequently used; last resort among methods; against only defiant actions
7. Emotive disposition	rod expresses parental love and anger (reasonable inference within Scripture)	spank only in love; no anger permitted

away from the rod (Bible) to an open palm or a broader instrument (the position of many of today's pro-spankers) is that it helps to distribute the impact more broadly across a wider surface and (in the case of an open palm) gives sensory feedback to the parent, all of which reduces markings and the possibility of injury. These two changes away from the biblical text move toward an improved disciplinary ethic. They are good changes inasmuch as they demonstrate greater care and concern for the long-term physical well-being of the child.

Such changes, though simple, constitute a dramatic ethical advancement beyond the concrete specificity of biblical teachings.

Likewise, the rationale for each of the other changes by contemporary pro-spankers can equally be summed up under the rubric of *a better or improved treatment of children.* They have moved away from the concrete-specific teaching of the Bible to a *kinder and gentler approach* to discipline. The graded reduction in number of strokes from forty maximum for teens (inferred from adult corporal punishment teaching within the Bible) to only two strokes maximum for young children and none permitted for teens (the position of today's pro-spankers) is due to concerns about excessive physical damage as well as the greater emphasis on reasoning capabilities of older children.[2] Thus relationship, reasoning and logical consequences (today's pro-spankers) completely replaces any practice of corporal punishment (Bible) for teenagers. Is the move a good one? Yes, it markedly advances a better treatment of children while still understanding the continuing need for disciplinary action within parent-child relationships. Yet again, the change away from seeing black-and-blue bruising marks as a virtue (Bible) to leaving no marks (today's pro-spankers) is done out of concern for the child's physical and emotional well-being, and because of a growing sensitivity to problems of abuse. Finally, reducing the frequency of spankings by reserving them for a specific type of high-handed infraction, using alternative noncorporal methods as a first resort (corporal punishment as a last resort) and replacing the "rod of anger" with a quiet and gentle parental disposition are in my estimation great changes, wonderful changes. Why? Because they evidence substantial ethical development in the right direction.

Could this ethical movement already present within the pro-spanker's contemporary position (relative to the concrete instructions of Scripture) be taken further even within a spanking framework?

---

[2]Andreas J. Köstenberger with David W. Jones, *God, Marriage and Family: Rebuilding the Biblical Foundation* (Wheaton, Ill.: Crossway, 2004), p. 161. Köstenberger argues that spanking may not work well with older children and that the older children get, the more reasoning ought to be emphasized. Of course, two smacks of physical discipline would simply be a joke to most teenagers. The reduced maximum number of allowed strokes in the beating (from where Scripture was) has pragmatically ruled out its feasibility for teenagers today.

Probably so. Further ethical development ought to be considered even for those who wish to stay with a pro-spanking approach. These further changes are simply logical extensions of the spirit contained in the seven changes that have already been introduced. For instance, it would make sense in today's context that Christian parents spank their kids within at least an ear-shot presence of a second adult who functions as an *accountability partner*. The adult accountability partner would ensure that all of the seven good departures from concrete-specific teachings of the Bible are in fact (not simply in theory) accomplished all of the time. Furthermore, Christian parents who advocate spanking might start reflecting on a set of self-imposed, partner-imposed and community-imposed disciplinary and remedial actions for their own lives, should they fail to live out this enacted ethic. In other words, today's pro-spanking ethic still has room for ethical improvements even if one chooses to stay within a corporal-punishment framework.[3]

In the remainder of this chapter I would like to provide my pro-spanking friends with a biblical basis for their journey beyond the concrete-specific teachings of the Bible in this area of corporal punishment. A biblical basis for their position can be established through an appeal to three areas of meaning within Scripture: (1) redemptive-movement meaning, (2) abstracted meaning and (3) purpose meaning. Each of these three avenues of biblical meaning is derived from within the corporal punishment texts themselves.

BIBLICAL BASIS 1: REDEMPTIVE-MOVEMENT MEANING

As someone might expect from having just read the slavery chapter,

---

[3]Someone might object that an adult accountability person is not logistically feasible, especially for single parents. However, this logistics objection can be easily overcome in a contemporary world where communication can take place through multiple mediums. Also, if need be, a cooling-down time for the adult administering the spanking might be a good idea. Should delay in discipline not fit with the short memory span of very young children, then a digital audio recording of the event would provide a record for one's accountability person. Unfortunately, I do not hear pro-spanking proponents calling for parental accountability, whether for their own sake as parents, for the sake of their children or for the sake of the Christian witness to a broader community. Nevertheless, such a development within a pro-spanking ethic coincides well with the spirit of the seven changes already made.

the first and most crucial biblical basis that supports the pro-spankers' moving "beyond" is Scripture's own redemptive-movement meaning. While pro-spankers do not themselves provide a biblical rationale for their "going beyond" application process, for the moment I would like to champion their cause. They have clearly moved to a better disciplinary ethic than the concrete "beatings with the rod" instructions of Scripture. Yet how are such dramatic ethical moves away from the Bible's concrete instructions actually biblical? There exists a valid biblical basis for this improved form of corporal punishment today through highlighting (1) the incremental nature of ethics in the Bible and (2) the redemptive spirit of Scripture—a component of meaning in the biblical text that is often overlooked. A logical extension of the *movement meaning* within the biblical text itself legitimizes their further two-smacks-max changes toward a better expression of a discipline ethic. I am simply asking readers to listen to the Bible as it is read within its larger social context of the ANE world. When we examine corporal punishment texts from other ancient Near Eastern countries, then we begin to hear something new and wonderful within the Bible. We hear the inspiring redemptive spirit of the biblical text.

Ancient Egyptian beatings: One hundred to two hundred blows. The New Kingdom period in Egypt (c. 1550-1069 B.C.E.) overlaps in time with the biblical exodus of Israel and their conquest of Canaan, whether calculating on the basis of an early or late departure from Egypt. Thus the following examples are especially pertinent since they overlap with Israel's closest contact to Egypt and with their firsthand experience of beatings in that foreign land (see Ex 2:11; 5:14, 16). The following is a sampling of typical court rulings during the New Kingdom period on crimes and their respective punishments, which often included beatings specified in terms of the number of strokes with the rod or whip:[4]

---

[4]For a detailed and helpful treatment see David Lorton, "The Treatment of Criminals in Ancient Egypt," in *The Treatment of Criminals in the Ancient Near East*, ed. J. M. Sasson (Leiden: Brill, 1977), pp. 2-64.

Crime	Punishment
unpaid land dues	100 strokes
seizure of a hide by a military person	100 blows and five open wounds[a]
civil administrators requisitioning state workers [for personal use]	200 blows, five open wounds and replacement of days lost
detention of a boat belonging to the royal foundation	200 blows, five open wounds and repayment of boat usage
interference with fishing or fowling	100 blows and five open wounds
driving a herdsman from his pasture	100 blows and five open wounds
stealing goods belonging to the royal foundation	100 blows, restored goods, and an additional 100-fold penalty

[a]We do not know if the five open wounds are part of or in addition to the beating.

As illustrated through this sample list of punishments, the extant Egyptian law codes provide at least two helpful insights. First, in the ancient Egyptian context a beating of one hundred blows is mentioned so frequently that it appears to function as something of a standard or typical beating. Nevertheless, a more severe beating could include as many as two hundred blows. Second, the matter of "five open wounds" demonstrates at least that such wounds, and not simply welts and bruises, were often a result of beatings (or possibly an added component). In this brutal beating context, it may come as a surprise to us today that for Egypt and for most of the ancient world physical beatings were actually "the mildest form of punishment."[5] Even more severe corporal punishments included torture, inhumane forms of death and mutilation of various body parts—cutting off the nose, eyes, ears, lips, hands, feet, breasts or genitals. These comparatively harsher punishments are often found within the ancient law codes (or legislative samplings) right next to penalties that involved physical beatings.

---

[5]A. G. McDowell, "Crime and Punishment," in *Encyclopedia of Ancient Egypt*, ed. D. B. Redford (Oxford: Oxford University Press, 2001), 1:318.

Ancient Babylonian beatings: Sixty blows. The Babylonian laws of Hammurabi (d. c. 1750) twice mention floggings, although the number of strokes is only stated in the latter of the following examples:

Crime	Punishment
false or unsupported accusation	flogging [number not specified] and shaving off half of person's hair
citizen striking the cheek of a higher class person	flogging in public with 60 stripes of an ox whip[a]

[a]See Martha T. Roth, *Law Collections from Mesopotamia and Asia Minor*, 2nd ed., Society of Biblical Literature Writings from the Ancient World 6 (Atlanta: Scholars Press, 1997), pp. 71-142. LH ¶¶ 127, 202. For a comprehensive source, see William W. Hallo and K. Lawson Younger Jr., eds. *The Context of Scripture*, vol. 2, *Monumental Inscriptions from the Biblical World* (Boston: Brill, 2003). A focused investigation of ancient-world punishments has recently been completed by Elisabeth Meier Tetlow, *Women, Crime, and Punishment in Ancient Law and Society*, vol. 1, *The Ancient Near East* (New York: Continuum, 2004), pp. 1-338.

In addition to floggings, however, the Babylonian law codes contain many penalties involving severe mutilation: cutting out the tongue, plucking out an eye, cutting off a hand, a breast, an ear or the nose.[6] Other physical punishments include being dragged around a field by cattle,[7] and the famous river ordeal, which may or may not have ended in death.[8] Given these other far harsher physical punishments, it is unlikely that we should understand sixty stripes as the maximum flogging penalty for ancient Babylonians. That sort of cap does not make much sense. But since the example of sixty strokes is the only specified number of strokes that we have, we will simply work with that figure.

Ancient Assyrian beatings: Five to one hundred blows. Middle Assyrian laws (c. 1076) provide an additional glimpse into the ancient Mesopotamian world of corporal punishment.[9]

---

[6]LH ¶¶ 127, 192-95, 205, 218, 226, 253, 282.

[7]LH ¶ 256.

[8]LH ¶¶ 132, 143. The river ordeal was where a person (often bound in some fashion) was thrown into a treacherous river. If they lived/survived, they were viewed as not guilty. But, if they died, they were seen as guilty and not by happenstance or fate but an act of punishment by the gods.

[9]See Martha T. Roth, *Law Collections from Mesopotamia and Asia Minor*, 2nd ed. (Atlanta: Scholars Press, 1997), pp. 153-209. Note especially MAL A ¶¶ 7, 18, 19, 40, 59; MAL B ¶¶ 7, 8, 9; MAL C ¶ 8; MAL F ¶ 1; MAL N ¶ 1; cf. MAPD ¶¶ 17, 18, 21. There are further examples where the number of lashes or strokes is either unclear or not specified (e.g., MAL B ¶¶ 14, 15, 18; MAL C ¶¶ 2, 3, 11; MAL E ¶ 1; MAL N ¶ 2).

Crime	Punishment
woman lays a hand on a man	20 blows with rods, 3,600 shekels of lead
unproven statements about a promiscuous wife: "everyone has sex with your wife"	40 blows, one month in the king's service, 3,600 shekels of lead
unproven rumors about a male being sodomized: "everyone sodomizes you"	50 blows, cut off hair, one month in king's service, 3,600 shekels of lead
striking a woman and causing her to abort her fetus	50 blows, one month service, 9,000 shekels of lead
prostitute wearing a veil ("available" women must be unveiled)	50 blows, pour hot tar over her head
a man not reporting a veiled prostitute or a veiled slave	50 blows, one month in king's service
a husband's right to punish his wife [unspecified offenses]	a man may whip his wife [unspecified number of blows], pluck out her hair, mutilate her ears and strike her
[offense unclear in text]	5 blows, 3,600 shekels of lead, one month in king's service
incorporating a large piece of property from a neighbor's field	100 blows, repay triple the land wrongly taken, cut off one finger, one month in king's service
incorporating a small piece of property from a neighbor's field	50 blows, repay triple the land wrongly taken, 3,600 shekels of lead, one month in king's service
building a well or permanent structure in another person's field	30 blows, forfeit the well or structure, 20 days in king's service
stealing an animal or other goods	50 blows, repay stolen goods, [x days] in king's service
stealing sheep [crime not entirely clear in the text]	100 blows, replace stolen sheep, tear out person's hair, one month service in king's service

As was the case in Egypt and Babylon, the Assyrian laws included mutilations such as gouging out eyes, castration ("turn him into a eunuch"), lacerating the face, pouring hot tar over the head, tearing out hair, cutting off fingers, hands, noses, ears and lips.[10] Once again, the river ordeal was also used as a punishment.[11]

Ancient Israel (the Bible): Forty blows maximum. The previous sketch of corporal punishment in the ancient world (Egyptian, Babylonian and Assyrian) uncovers a crucial element of meaning within the biblical text. When the words of Scripture are read within this ancient context, we "hear" its redemptive spirit. We begin to sense a wonderful redemptive trend within the Bible that ought to excite and inspire Christians. Let's go back again and look at the text of Deuteronomy 25:1-3, which was raised earlier in chapter one. Within this text notice the maximum number of lashes and the stated rationale:

> When men have a dispute, they are to take it to court and the judges will decide the case, acquitting the innocent and condemning the guilty. If the guilty man deserves to be beaten, the judge shall make him lie down and have him flogged in his presence with the number of lashes his crime deserves, but he must not give him more than *forty lashes*. If he is flogged more than that, *your brother will be degraded in your eyes.* (NIV, italics added)

As we read this text within a larger ancient framework where "justice" often included beatings with upwards to two hundreds lashes or strokes, various horrendous bodily mutilations and other torturous means of punishment, then the biblical text speaks with fresh insight. Within this sort of brutal and harsh world, Deuteronomy 25:1-3 (1) limits corporal punishment of adults to a maximum of forty strokes, (2) requires that the number of lashes be proportionate to the offense—indicating a lesser amount for lesser infractions, and (3) explicitly states concern for limiting the number of lashes because otherwise "your neighbor will degraded in your sight." When the corporal punishment

---

[10]MAL A ¶¶ 4, 5, 8, 9, 15, 20, 24, 40, 44, 59; MAL B ¶ 8; MAL F ¶¶ 1, 2; cf. MAPD ¶ 21.
[11]MAL A ¶¶ 22, 24.

text of Deuteronomy 25:1-3 is read within the larger ANE social context, the redemptive-movement meaning is huge. The biblical text moves the covenant people of God toward a *kinder and gentler* administration of justice and toward a *greater dignity* for the human being who is punished—this is the spirit of the Bible as it is read within its larger social framework.

Christians need to recognize that at one level biblical instructions do not always represent an ultimate ethic in their treatment of human beings. To think that they do is a misguided assumption. But perhaps the greater problem is not realizing or sensing the redemptive spirit of the text and thus failing to let that biblical brilliance and passion ignite our hearts today. Staying with the concrete specificity on the page is like trying to do ethics today with museum pieces that come from an archaeological dig—they are fragile, eroded and strangely out of place. However, fusing our spirits with the spirit of Scripture and thinking creatively about how we might allow Scripture's movement meaning or redemptive spirit to be fleshed out today is a wonderful and invigorating task.

So, let us be thankful for what two-smacks-max pro-spankers have done. They have moved beyond the concrete-specific or "on the page" teaching of the Bible to a much better enacted ethic—one which embraces a greater fulfillment of the Bible's spirit and redemptive movement. My only question is, Why stop here? Couldn't this same spirit be taken logically to an even greater fulfillment? Chapters four and five address these sorts of lingering questions.

Someone might object that I have engaged a redemptive-movement reading of Scripture at the level of *adult* corporal punishment themes and yet I have applied its insights in our contemporary context to today's ethical debate about disciplining *children*. Fair enough. Yes, I am drawing an inference from what is going on in terms of redemptive movement at the adult level of the Bible's corporal punishment texts for how we should move in our application of the child corporal punishment texts. But I suggest that the inference is a reasonable one. Criminal punishments in the ANE community often provided an overlapping interaction or crossover between the community and what went on in the home.[12] Look for instance at the seventh Assyrian example (see p. 82) that gives the husband a wide range of punishments for his wife, including that of physical beatings. It is reasonable to assume that an Assyrian husband who functioned within the "published" community law standards would be considered within the accepted societal norms when delivering a beating by the rod or whip to his wife. Accordingly, the reduced Israelite published maximum of forty lashes, when compared to the Egyptian, Babylonian and Assyrian scenes, would have had an immediate effect on corporal punishment within the home. It is entirely reasonable to expect the redemptive-movement meaning within Israel's published community standards (relative to its social context) to affect corporal discipline within the home—directly for adult wives and in a scaled-down sense for children—especially as we consider the biblical emphasis on greater dignity of the person combined with a kinder and gentler approach.[13]

BIBLICAL BASIS 2: ABSTRACTED MEANING

The second biblical basis for pro-spankers journeying beyond the concrete-specific teaching in the Bible is founded in the *abstracted* meaning of the text. Perhaps I can best explain this by talking about what might be considered bad abstracted meaning and, conversely, some examples of good abstracted meaning. Here is the negative side. Preachers sometimes talk about the underlying principle of the text

---

[12]I might add that the involvement at times of the injured party in extracting justice (the blood or compensatory avenger) also brought the community law standards into the home setting. As a third overlap I can add the heavily blurred categories in ANE law of criminal and civil procedures that are distinct parts of our legal proceedings. The distinction is not completely unknown in the ancient world but overlap of these categories is considerable.

[13]Fortunately, nothing within the Scriptures explicitly establishes any right of a husband to physically discipline his wife. However, this is not to say that corporal punishment of wives did not take place in Israel. Nor is it to say that discretionary corporal punishment of wives cannot be seen as a valid prerogative (even responsibility) of the husband from the inferred values of various Old Testament texts (e.g., note the implied physical punishment in Hos 2:2-3 and Ezek 16:32-40). Such arguments have certainly been part of church history. While hard to fathom from our present horizon, at one point Christians actually debated the legitimacy of a husband's right to physically discipline his wife (see Anthony Fletcher, "The Protestant Idea of Marriage in Early Modern England," in *Religion, Culture and Society in Early Modern Britain*, ed. Anthony Fletcher and Peter Roberts [Cambridge: Cambridge University Press, 1994], pp. 161-81). Regarding children, see the discussion of a scaled-down or proportional framework discussed in chap. 1.

almost as if it were an entity apart from the text itself that magically lies below the surface; the preaching task is to figure out what the underlying principle is.[14] A bad example of the underlying-principle approach is when a pastor uses the Joseph story in Genesis to extract from that story *itself* biblical principles about the handling of anger based on Joseph forgiving his brothers and other relational elements in the story. Personally, I do not think that the Joseph narratives in Genesis were ever intended (authorial intent) to teach principles about handling anger and jealousy. Yes, they could be used as an *illustration* of anger principles properly derived from other biblical texts. But this is a bad example of abstracted meaning because it is not legitimately derived from the text. Our primary caution in the area of abstracted meaning, then, is to say that it must be tied into the authorial intent of the text.

On the other hand, there is such a thing as good abstracted meaning. This good abstracted meaning is more tightly tied to the words of the text and to the authorial intent of that text. Good abstracted meaning is actually embedded in the very concrete-specific words themselves. While there are safeguards and qualifiers (as already mentioned), readers should not be locked into rigid specificity. In general, there is often an element of *abstracted meaning* within the norms of everyday discourse between people. In a moment I will illustrate this within an example of a parent giving his or her child instructions, and make the point that biblical hermeneutics is not that much different with respect to understanding abstracted meaning.

A classic "cleaning the garage" story may help illustrate. Here is an everyday example of a parent giving instructions to a teenager to "sweep out the garage." Within our own family context this kind of instruction might well have been given to our teenaged son Joel when he was fourteen years old. Let's say that one afternoon I call my son to the garage and hand him a broom with the explicit instruction, "Joel, here's a broom; please sweep out the garage. I'll come back in an hour and check your job. Thanks." Now, suppose I come back an hour later and

---

[14]This is why I generally use the expression "abstracted meaning" rather than underlying principles. The idea of abstracted meaning must be rooted in the authorial intent and the words of the biblical text as reflected within that intent.

the garage is still messy; nothing has been done. I find my teenager sitting with his feet up on a bench, headphones blasting, and he is playing air-guitar with the broom instead of cleaning the garage. In all likelihood this is a case of youthful disobedience—clear and simple!

But here is a second scenario. Suppose that I return to the garage and find that it is wonderfully clean far beyond my expectations. I watch as my son Joel finishes putting away the shop vacuum that he has carried up from the basement because he knew that he could do a better job cleaning the garage with the shop vacuum than with the broom. A good father would never accuse his son of disobedience and say, "Look, I told you to use a broom!" Of course not. Rather, a good father would commend his son for taking the initiative to use a better method for fulfilling the abstracted meaning within his instructions. Joel had obviously caught that my abstracted meaning was "clean the garage," while my concrete-specific instruction was, "Here's a broom; sweep out the garage." As with obeying parental directives, if one fulfills the abstracted meaning within Scripture's imperatives, such a move logically provides a solid biblical basis for going beyond the concrete-specific instructions of the Bible.

Now consider a somewhat humorous example of how Christians often move quickly away from the concrete-specific meaning of the Bible's instructions and embrace the abstracted meaning of the text. Here I will post two proverbs side by side and ask, What exactly does the Bible teach?

Proverbs 22:15	Proverbs 31:6-7
Folly is bound up	Give *beer* to those who are perishing,
in the heart of a boy,	*wine* to those who are in anguish;
but the *rod* of discipline	let them drink [beer and wine]
drives it far away.	and forget their poverty
	and remember their misery no more. (NIV)

If we ponder Proverbs 31:6-7 for a while, it becomes apparent that there are different and often better ways of fulfilling the abstracted meaning within that text than the particulars expressed in the concrete text. For instance, morphine might be much better than alcohol to give people who are dying and in physical agony. On the other hand, providing beer and wine to those in emotional anguish or poverty is problematic: (1) they may become dependent on alcohol to "fix" their broken worlds and eventually become addicted, and (2) they most likely would benefit from not just a temporary relief from poverty or emotional anguish but from a more lasting or durable relief.

Figure 3.1 diagrams the abstracted meaning within Proverbs 31:6-7 in a manner that shows it moving up the ladder of abstraction.

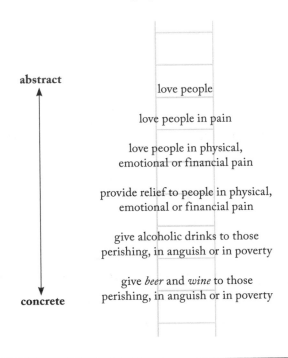

abstract

love people

love people in pain

love people in physical, emotional or financial pain

provide relief to people in physical, emotional or financial pain

give alcoholic drinks to those perishing, in anguish or in poverty

give *beer* and *wine* to those perishing, in anguish or in poverty

concrete

Figure 3.1. The abstracted meaning within Proverbs 31:6-7

In this example of good abstracted meaning, we could argue that each of these levels of abstracted meaning is embedded within the concrete-specific text itself. It should be evident from this example that Christian obedience to the biblical text is not "more biblical" if one obeys the actual words on the page in all of their rugged, earthy specificity. Rather, devout followers of Christ are often "more biblical" when reflecting on a verse and recognizing how they could live out its abstracted meaning in better ways today. In other words, providing morphine for the pain experienced by someone dying and building affordable housing for the poor are in many cases a far *better* means of fulfilling the abstracted meaning within Proverbs 31:6-7 than handing out cans of beer.

Even so, let's applaud the advances made by contemporary two-smacks-max people in their clear movement toward a gentler and kinder type of discipline. Yes, they have modified and gone beyond numerous aspects of the Bible's concrete instructions about corporal punishment. But they have done well. In addition to movement meaning, abstracted meaning within the biblical text provides an excellent biblical basis for pro-spankers' "going beyond" journey. Regardless of our positions on corporal punishment, let's celebrate this good feature within their biblical application. They are still enacting the abstracted meaning of the Bible despite their departure from its "on the page" or face-value instructions.

Before turning to the third aspect of biblical meaning that supports going beyond the concrete corporal punishment instructions of the Bible, let me again reiterate the viewpoint of this chapter. These are *my* hermeneutical suggestions; I frankly do not know how two-smacks-max proponents are going to respond. I am offering these as reasonable solutions for resolving the problems outlined in chapter one. Those writing from a two-smacks-max position have been silent about their departure from Scripture. So, this is my attempt to open the conversation about how to understand and apply the Bible. Without a hermeneutical approach at least something *like* the one I am suggesting, I honestly do not know how two-smacks-max spankers can in a credible fashion move from what the text actually says (its sevenfold teaching) to their own (quite different) position. I do not want to infer that the hermeneutical journey will be easy. On the other hand, I do not know how else to resolve their hermeneutical inconsistencies and address some of the troubling components within the corporal punishment texts.

BIBLICAL BASIS 3: PURPOSE MEANING

A third biblical basis for pro-spankers taking their application beyond the concrete-specific teaching of Scripture is founded in the *purpose* meaning of the text. In the case of biblical corporal-punishment texts the stated goals of the beatings with a rod are (1) [negatively] to turn children from folly, and (2) [positively] to help them embrace wisdom. Surely these are good purposes. In a moment I will argue that fulfilling these purposes using alternative means, despite departing from biblical instructions at the concrete-specific level, is also good and appropriate biblical obedience. Once again, a person's behavior is not necessarily more biblical simply because he or she more closely replicates the concrete level of meaning in the biblical text.

Before affirming purpose meaning in a legitimate role, let me caution against its improper or fallacious use. Most Christian ethicists agree, as well as many secular ethicists for that matter, that the purpose or ends of an action should never be used to justify the action whether biblical or otherwise. "The end justifies the means" is a common fallacy among misguided Christian attempts to rescue troubling biblical texts.[15] In the final analysis it does not matter how lofty our purposes or goals are; such good ends never justify the means taken to achieve them. In the case of biblical "beatings with a rod," the stated goals of helping a child live wisely and avoid folly are good. Nevertheless, they hardly legitimize the means of physical beatings with the rod or whip in order to achieve them. The ends or goals never justify how we get there. For instance, physical torture or physical mutilation could theoretically be used instead of physical beatings to produce similar behavior modified actions in children or adults. But this does not legitimize using torture or mutilation—it really does not matter how pristine our purposes may be.

Due to the prevalent misuse of purpose meaning within Scripture, let me further clarify exactly what I am and am not saying. By appealing to purpose meaning, I am not saying that purpose meaning automatically validates the ethical status of all noncorporal methods of discipline that we will explore later (see chap. 5 and the postscript) any more than purpose meaning justifies corporal methods of discipline.

---

[15]See my work *Brutal, Bloody and Barbaric: War Texts That Trouble the Soul* (Downers Grove, Ill.: InterVarsity Press, forthcoming) for an extensive critique of this sort of fallacious Christian reasoning.

Such an ethical assessment of methods must be made on their own merit and on the basis of comparison between methods. However, provided that alternative noncorporal methods of discipline *can* achieve the two stated biblical purposes (avoiding folly and embracing wisdom), then they fulfill an important part of the biblical concern for discipline in the first place. Thus the achievement of stated purposes for an action provides an important biblical basis for embracing other noncorporal methods. This aspect of meaning provides yet another crucial avenue for assessing whether we have gone beyond the concrete-specific teachings of the Bible *biblically*.

Should we be inclined to depart from the concrete-specific teaching of the Bible and embrace noncorporal forms of discipline only, then the Bible's stated *purpose meaning* does provide a legitimate basis for such a departure. For example, let's say that the twofold stated purpose of physical beatings—avoiding folly and embracing wise living—could be achieved through some alternative expressions of noncorporal discipline. If this is the case, then a Christian's alternative disciplinary methods may well depart from the "beat children with the rod" instructions of the Bible but should still be seen as biblical in the sense that they accomplish the purpose meaning of the text.

Along the same line of reasoning, we should commend our two-smacks-max spanking advocates for their pronounced departure from the Bible. True, they have not embraced the sole use of noncorporal methods. But they have moved away from seven key concrete components of what the Bible teaches either explicitly or implicitly about corporal punishment. Does this mean that their views are any less biblical? No, not at all. In addition to realizing movement meaning and abstract meaning, they also still fulfill the text's purpose meaning. Furthermore, inasmuch as their changes represent an improved disciplinary ethic beyond the Bible's concrete-specific teachings, they have in fact become more (not less) biblical in their child-rearing practices—a delightful irony indeed!

CONCLUSION

Today's two-smacks-max spanking advocates have departed markedly from the concrete-specific teachings of the Bible. They have chosen not to embrace what the Bible instructs either explicitly or implicitly on the subject of corporal punishment regarding age limitations, number of lashes, bodily location of the beatings, the virtue of resultant wounds and marks, the nature of the striking instrument, the broad-based type of infractions for its usage, and the emotive state of the parent administering the spanking. Nevertheless, their reasons for making these changes away from the Bible are sane and reasonable. In general, the changes come under the rubric of a *kinder and gentler treatment of children* while still achieving discipline.

What the loving and gentle Dobson-type pro-spankers are lacking, however, is a biblical basis for their changes. How can they say they are actually doing what the Bible teaches when they have departed so markedly from the Bible? This chapter seeks to provide my pro-spanking friends with a biblical basis for their approach to disciplining children. Moreover, this chapter has also argued that a Christian is not necessarily more biblical simply because he or she replicates the biblical text more closely in terms of its concrete particulars. This is a widespread misconception. Ironically, we become more biblical at times by departing from the Bible in terms of its particulars! Within the corporal punishment texts themselves there exists three crucial components of meaning—movement, abstract and purpose—that provide a solid biblical basis for departing from a text's concrete-specific level of meaning.

Consequently, we should celebrate what today's kind and gentle pro-spankers have done in their courageous journey to a new world—an ocean's distance away from where faith communities of the distant past would surely have landed. They have changed the face of how Christian parents discipline their kids. I think they have rightly forged a better and more developed disciplinary ethic that fulfills in far greater fashion the unrealized ethic of the Bible itself. In so doing, they have in fact taken the Bible's *redemptive-movement meaning* to an entirely new level of fulfillment—a text like Deuteronomy 25:1-3 cries out for kinder and gentler disciplinary actions, especially when read within its ancient social world. They have also remained faithful to and developed better ways of expressing the *abstracted meaning* of the text (discipline) in a manner not unlike our garage-cleaning story. Finally, they have introduced these departures from the biblical text while still fulfilling its explicit *purpose meaning*, namely, helping children turn from folly and embrace wise living.

I am genuinely pleased with the more loving and gentle two-smacks-max movement as it has sought to frame an improved disciplinary ethic. Nevertheless, after reading this chapter on the threefold biblical basis for going beyond, I am left wondering about a few unresolved questions. Is it possible to journey further? Should we journey further? Can a Christian parent be faithful to the teachings of Scripture about disciplining children and nevertheless use only noncorporal methods? Could these three areas of biblical meaning—movement meaning, abstract meaning and purpose meaning—also provide a biblical basis for using only noncorporal approaches to discipline? Chapters four and five and the postscript (through a parenting story) will explore these lingering questions.

PART III

Lingering Questions

4

WHAT ABOUT ADULT
CORPORAL PUNISHMENT?

Not too long ago I gave a public address on how Christian pro-spankers today have moved well beyond the Bible—it covered the seven ways discussed in chapter one. Following the lecture a pastor came up to me and suggested that perhaps in light of clear biblical teaching, we ought to bring back the use of corporal punishment for adults. Since the Bible unquestionably teaches the "rod and whip" for adults, this gentleman, at least for sake of argument, was ready to advocate a return to adult corporal punishment within our society and justice system. This comeback question was not entirely unexpected.[1] In response I asked how he felt about using a heavy knife or an ax to chop off someone's hand. Was he comfortable with that form of corporal punishment within Scripture? Interestingly, this Christian leader was not so quick to endorse hand amputation or mutilation as a punishment for adults today.

Although this book's development of corporal punishment in the Bible has focused primarily on the "rod and whip" texts of Scripture, a fuller understanding of corporal punishment in the Bible must also include the "heavy knife" within that portrait. Any discussion about what the Bible says about corporal punishment needs to wrestle with three stark instruments: the rod, the whip and the heavy knife. There is a

---

[1]In a similar fashion a few Christians, after reading *Slaves, Women and Homosexuals*, have become convinced that we should once again permit slavery. Fortunately, this "let us head back" represents a very small minority of Christians.

good reason why this third component of the trilogy—the heavy knife—makes for a fitting finish. Among other things, the hand-amputation passage of Deuteronomy 25:11-12 provides a huge dose of reality in our ethical reflections about the rod and whip within Scripture. At the very least it illustrates the range of severity within the corporal punishment instructions of the Bible. For those who invoke the Bible as the basis for spanking children today and, correspondingly, in at least a hypothetical sense are prepared to return to the rod and whip for adults upon reading this book thus far, I would ask them about Deuteronomy 25:11-12. Are they open to accepting the full range of adult corporal punishment within Scripture? Are they willing to cut off a wife's hand today? And if not, it might be of benefit to consider why they are not so predisposed.[2] The discussion that follows provides a biblical rationale for such intuitions.

This chapter unfolds in four parts. First, we will examine Deuteronomy 25:11-12 in order to work through various interpretive options. I will argue briefly for the traditional view that Deuteronomy 25:11-12 calls for the hand amputation of a wife because of the loss of progeny or procreative abilities for an injured male. In this section we will also explore why such a text sounds so bizarre and out of sync within our contemporary world. Second, we will examine a series of ANE mutilation texts to see just how pervasive the legal penalty of corporal mutilation was in the ancient world. We need to sense the brutality that was typical of ancient justice in order to hear the biblical text correctly. Third, having set the ancient-world backdrop, we will be able to appreciate ways in which Deuteronomy 25:11-12, as repulsive as it is for most contemporary audiences, was redemptive within its original setting. Yes, there is redemptive movement even in this text! The movement is incremental within its ancient environment and thus yearns for us to carry its redemptive spirit further to an ultimate ethical application. Fourth, we come back to our opening question: What about corporal punishment for adults today? After a lengthy tour through the messy and grotesque world of ANE bodily mutilations,

---

[2]While some Islamic groups favor hand amputation (and worse) today, this is hardly true for most present-day followers of Jesus.

we will be better prepared to give sober and thoughtful reflection to our opening question.

THE HEAVY KNIFE (HAND AMPUTATION) TEXT

The text of Deuteronomy 25:11-12 describes a fight between two males where the wife of one intervenes in an attempt to save her husband by grabbing the genitals of her husband's opponent. As a result, the wife is subject to an extremely harsh punishment, namely, the amputation of her hand:

> If two men are fighting and the wife of one of them comes to rescue her husband from his assailant, and she reaches out and seizes him by his private parts, *you shall cut off her hand.* Show her no pity. (NIV, italics added)

Please pause and reread this biblical text. The words "you shall cut off her hand" are hardly pleasant to the ear. Even more hideous is the visual version. Imagine seeing this portrayed in a movie—you would shrink and turn away. How much more grotesque it would be to view in person the cutting off a woman's hand as such an event would unfold in a live setting. The mind is powerful and the sequence of images leaves one stunned.

Most Christians have no idea that Deuteronomy 25:11-12 is even in the Bible. When speaking about this "meat cleaver" passage and the full range of corporal punishment texts in Scripture, I often take a twenty-dollar bill and tape it to my laptop for everyone to see. Then, I ask if anyone in the audience has either preached this Deuteronomy text or heard it preached. If they have, I invite them to see me afterward and the money is theirs. On this Deuteronomy passage and on several other corporal punishment texts discussed within this book, I have never lost a dime! This exercise drives home how we as Christians can easily enter into a discussion about corporal punishment in the Bible without knowing what that really entails. If we advocate (for sake of argument) a return to adult corporal punishment in our contemporary setting based on plain, face-value biblical teaching, then perhaps we ought to include the whole of biblical teaching on the subject of corporal punishment, not just part of it. Here is the central point of this chapter: *Christians cannot entertain a return to the rod and whip for adults without wrestling long and hard with the heavy knife.*

We can appreciate why this text is rarely, if ever, preached today. The passage troubles present-day readers because it is completely out of sync with our world and raises thorny ethical questions. The severity of the punishment for the intervening wife—the amputation of her hand—seems extremely harsh and even barbaric. In our world kicking or injuring an attacker's groin is an accepted part of a smart response for someone under physical attack. It immobilizes the attacker with pain. Our legal system and courts view such self-defense actions as reasonable force. Our martial arts schools teach children and adults alike to use such genital-directed force as an acceptable way of protection in the case of physical assault. Should someone else's life or physical well being be at risk, we would not think twice about a person with lesser capabilities (generally the case with a woman entering a fight between two men) using these tactics to free the endangered person. We would probably applaud her heroic act, which might have put her own life in danger. Such a text baffles our sense of justice, and even if there is a negative outcome for the male opponent, we shudder at the thought of chopping off the woman's "helping hand."

Some scholars have proposed an alternative interpretation, namely, that Deuteronomy 25:11-12 requires the cutting off of the woman's genitals or her genital hair.[3] Such recent proposals are possible reconstructions, but the weight of the lexical evidence is much stronger in support of the traditional hand-amputation view, namely, that the text commands the cutting off of a wife's hand.[4] For the purposes of this

---

[3]Lyle Eslinger, "The Case of an Immodest Lady Wrestler in Deuteronomy XXV 11-12," *Vestus Testamentum* 31, no. 3 (1981): 269-81; and Jerome T. Walsh, "'You Shall Cut Off Her . . . Palm?' A Reexamination of Deuteronomy 25:11-12," *Journal of Semitic Studies* 49 (2004): 47-58.

[4]Marc Cortez, "The Law on Violent Intervention: Deuteronomy 25.11-12 Revisited," *Journal for the Study of the Old Testament* 30, no. 3 (2006): 431-47. Cf. Eugene H. Merrill, *Deuteronomy*, NAC (Nashville: Broadman & Holman, 1994), p. 329; Anthony Phillips, *Deuteronomy* (Cambridge: Cambridge University Press, 1973), p. 170; Ian Cairns, *Word and Presence: A Commentary on the Book of Deuteronomy*, ITC (Grand Rapids: Eerdmans, 1992), p. 218; Peter Craigie, *The Book of Deuteronomy*, NICOT (Grand Rapids: Eerdmans, 1976), p. 316; Dennis T. Olson, *Deuteronomy and the Death of Moses: A Theological Reading*, OBT (Minneapolis: Fortress, 1994),

chapter, I will understand Deuteronomy 25:11-12 along these traditional and more persuasive lines. Furthermore, while not explicitly
stated, the primary concern or offense appears to be that of injuring the
assailant's testicles to the extent that he is unable to procreate. The loss
of progeny is likely the crux aspect of the crime for several reasons.
First, there is a close parallel in Middle Assyrian laws with comparable
overlapping components: a similar fighting context, a woman damaging a man's testicles and the penalty of corporal mutilation for the
woman. As will be argued later, the portion of the Assyrian law that
most closely compares with the biblical example is the complete "two
testicle" damage to the male ability to procreate (note italics portion of
the Assyrian text):

> If a woman should crush a man's testicle during a quarrel, they shall cut
> off one of her fingers. And even if the physician should bandage it, but *the
> second testicle then becomes infected, . . . or if she should crush the second testicle
> during the quarrel—they shall gouge out both of her [eyes or her breasts].*[5]

As with the biblical text, this Assyrian law combines the crime of a
woman grabbing a man's genitals and the punishment of body mutilation. The Assyrian law makes the loss of male progeny explicit.[6] Damage to the male's procreative ability thus appears to be a shared underlying component that would have been obvious within that legal-world
setting. In other words, there was no need to make the loss of procreative ability explicit in the biblical text; it would likely have been well

---

pp. 111-12; Christopher Wright, *Deuteronomy*, NIBC (Peabody, Mass.: Hendrickson, 1996),
pp. 266-67.
[5]MAL A ¶ 4. The translation is from Martha T. Roth, *Law Collections from Mesopotamia and
Asia Minor*, 2nd ed. Society of Biblical Literature Writings from the Ancient World 6 (Atlanta:
Scholars Press, 1997), pp. 156-57.
[6]For a brief introduction to Assyrian law codes in the ANE context, see Kenton L. Sparks,
Ancient Texts for the Study of the Hebrew Bible: A Guide to the Background Literature (Peabody,
Mass.: Hendrickson, 2005), pp. 424-25; John H. Walton, *Ancient Near Eastern Thought and the
Old Testament: Introducing the Conceptual World of the Hebrew Bible* (Grand Rapids: Baker,
2006), pp. 69-71, 287-302; Raymond Westbrook and Bruce Wells, *Everyday Law in Biblical
Israel: An Introduction* (Louisville: Westminster John Knox, 2009), pp. 9-34, 69-89. For an in-
depth discussion, see Daniel C. Snell, ed., *A Companion to the Ancient Near East* (Malden,
Mass.: Blackwell, 2007); Raymond Westbrook, Bruce Wells and F. Rachel Magdalene, eds.,
Law from the Tigris to the Tiber: The Writings of Raymond Westbrook (Winona Lake, Ind.: Eisenbrauns, 2009).

understood already. Second, the verses immediately before Deuteronomy 25:11-12 (vv. 5-10) are all about the loss of progeny—they develop the case of a brother's responsibility to help in fathering a son for a widow without children. A brother must be willing to help build up his brother's family line and thereby remove the danger that the name of the dead brother would be "blotted out" of the land of Israel. This contextual concern for securing progeny and not damaging another person's ability to sire children and carry on the family name, even if by proxy, significantly increases the probability that Deuteronomy 25:11-12 implicitly addresses damage to a man's ability to father children. On contextual grounds, therefore, it seems highly probable that the injured male in this amputation text can no longer produce offspring.[7] Third, the severity of the penalty in verse 12 (cutting off a wife's hand) further argues that the woman's actions have incurred serious and lasting damages to the male's ability to procreate. Within its ancient-world context only this degree of permanent damage to the testicles (not simply the shame of touching male genitals) sufficiently explains the permanent and extreme nature of the punishment.[8] While the biblical text does not offer a legal ruling on partial damages (one testicle), the related concern for progeny within Deuteronomy 25 seems to make complete inability of male reproduction (two testicles damaged) the most probable crime within the comparison.

Given this understanding of Deuteronomy 25:11-12 (hand amputation for damages that incurred loss of procreative ability), we now need

---

[7]Each of the commentators in footnote 4 (of this chap.) make the connection to progeny within a contextual reading of Deut 25:11-12. Biddle further proposes a stronger relationship between 25:11-12 and its preceding context, namely, that the sandal retaliation against a "brother" who would not help restore a brother's name in Israel was to be limited—in the case of an ensuing fight, the offended sister-in-law was not to damage his genitals in a retaliatory action (see Mark E. Biddle, *Deuteronomy*, SHBC [Macon, Ga.: Smyth & Helwys, 2003], pp. 372-75). Rofé highlights the contextual concern for progeny by drawing attention to the converse idea of the Amalekite's name being blotted out (Deut 25:17-19) and the two weights in a sack (Deut 25:13-16) having a double entendre with the male's genitals of the previous law. The contextual focus on fertility and progeny may be more emphatic than a casual reader might catch (see Alexander Rofé, *Deuteronomy: Issues and Interpretation*, OTS [New York: T & T Clark, 2002], pp. 65-67).

[8]Some readers might think that the *potential* of genital damage itself was the crime of the intervening wife. This interpretation is highly improbable in view of (1) the strength of the punishment, and (2) the fact that elsewhere within Scripture only *actual* (not potential) damages are given punishments.

to walk through ancient Near Eastern legal texts in order to discover the degree to which they utilize mutilation as a punishment. Gaining a feel for the practice of mutilation within the broader ancient world helps us appreciate the comparative restraint of Scripture.

ANE MUTILATION TEXTS

There is no better way to engage the mutilation text of Deuteronomy 25:11-12 than to see it within its ancient-world setting where mutilation texts were far more common than one might think. This survey of ANE mutilation texts from Sumer, Egypt, Babylon, Assyria and Anatolia provides a fascinating journey into a world of bodily punishments that seem almost unbelievable to the contemporary reader.

Sumerian mutilation laws. We start with something of an anomaly. For the most part Sumerian law codes (c. 2100-1930 B.C.E.) seldom utilize corporal mutilation as a punishment. The two cases where it does occur are at least worth noting.

Crime	Punishment
real estate theft	peg driven through his or her mouth
a woman's offensive speech to a man	teeth smashed with bricks[a]

[a]See Elisabeth Meier Tetlow, *Women, Crime, and Punishment in Ancient Law and Society*, vol. 1, The *Ancient Near East* (New York: Continuum, 2004), p. 9.

It is difficult to know how to view the relative lack of mutilation within the Sumerian laws. We are missing large sections of these law codes; the available portion represents only about one third of the whole document for one code, and an undetermined amount is missing from a second code.[9] Given that corporal mutilation does occur in Sumerian texts (the two examples cited here), perhaps the fuller law codes, if we

---

[9]Of the two most well-known Sumerian legal codes, the Laws of Lipit-Ishtar has extant only 400 of the original 1200 lines (approximately 2/3 of the document or roughly 800 lines are missing) and the Laws of Ur-Namma are broken in a spot that leaves us unable to determine how much of that document (1/3? 2/3?) is missing (see Kenton L. Sparks, *Ancient Texts for the Study of the Hebrew Bible: A Guide to the Background Literature* [Peabody, Mass.: Hendrickson, 2005], pp. 419-20).

had them, would have provided us with other such instances. Or possibly we have a legal tradition that like the biblical corpus is moving away from corporal mutilations within its application of justice. The evidence is too scant to speculate.

Egyptian mutilation laws. The New Kingdom period in Egypt (c. 1550-1069 B.C.E.) overlaps nicely in time with the biblical events from pre-exodus days until the time of King David. Thus documents from this time period provide a particularly helpful window through which to view Israel's law codes. During these years Israel would have experienced Egypt firsthand and would have seen the impact of its mutilation laws. While the mutilation penalty of inflicting "open wounds" is extremely frequent within the Egyptian texts, for the sake of brevity I will cite only one example. If all of these open-wound cases were added, I could easily triple the list. Similarly, there are repeated mutilation laws within Egyptian legal documents that speak of cutting off a person's nose and ears along with their being sent to Kush, a forced labor camp. Although numerous perjury cases contain this "mutilation plus Kush" punishment, I will likewise cite such cases only once. As can be seen in the sampling of court rulings here, cutting off of ears and noses along with inflicting open wounds was a standard part of Egyptian corporal punishments.[10]

Crime	Punishment
encroaching on field boundaries	cut off nose and ears and make person a cultivator
stealing an animal belonging to royal foundation	cut off nose and ears and make person a cultivator
harem conspiracy	cut off nose and ears[a]
speaking falsehood (i.e., perjury)	cut off nose and ears and send to Kush [frequently recorded punishment]

[10]For a detailed treatment see David Lorton, "The Treatment of Criminals in Ancient Egypt," in *The Treatment of Criminals in the Ancient Near East*, ed. J. M. Sasson (Leiden: Brill, 1977), pp. 2-64.

Crime	Punishment
stolen goods	unspecified mutilation
oaths of witnesses if found lying	unspecified mutilation
theft of tomb goods	cut off nose and ears and 50 open wounds
repeated offense of libel	cut off nose and ears

[a]In this group conspiracy 1/3 were executed, 1/3 forced to commit suicide and 1/3 mutilated (cutting off nose and ears).

Babylonian mutilation laws. The well-known Babylonian code of Hammurabi (c. 1750 B.C.E.) contains penalties that often include rather severe mutilation: cutting out the tongue, plucking out an eye, cutting off a hand, a breast, an ear or the nose. The following are some prominent examples.[11]

Crime	Punishment
adopted child disowns parents ("you are not my father/mother")	cut out child's tongue
adopted child runs away to real father/mother	pluck out child's eye
wet nurse takes on contracts for more than one child and child dies	cut off her breast
child strikes his father	cut off child's hand
slave strikes a free person	cut off slave's hand
physician in surgery blinds or causes death	cut off physician's hand
barber shaves off slave's hairlock without owner's permission	cut off the barber's hand
hired man steals seed or fodder	cut off his hand
hired man steals seed for field and cannot repay harvest equivalent	drag man around field by cattle [may cause mutilation or death]

---

[11]LH ¶¶ 192-95, 205, 218, 226, 253, 256, 282. See Roth, *Law Collections from Mesopotamia and Asia Minor*, pp. 71-142. LH ¶¶ 127 and 202.

Crime	Punishment
slave challenges authority of his master	cut off slave's ear
breach of contract[a] [contracts often mandated mutilation for breaking them]	amputate nose, shave half of the head, stretch out arms, parade around city

[a]Tetlow, *Women, Crime, and Punishment*, p. 97.

Assyrian mutilation laws. As a contemporary with the biblical text, Middle Assyrian laws (c. 1363-1057 B.C.E.) provide yet another helpful window into the ancient Mesopotamian world of crime and punishment. Once again we discover that corporal mutilation functions as an important component of penalties within Assyrian legal codes. As with Egypt and Babylon, the Assyrian laws and palace decrees include excessive bodily mutilations such as gouging out eyes, castration ("turn him into a eunuch"), lacerating the face, pouring hot tar over the head, tearing out hair, cutting off fingers, hands, noses, ears or lips.[12]

Crime	Punishment
a slave steals goods from his/her owner	cut off slave's nose and ears
a wife steals from a neighbor	return goods and the husband cuts off his wife's ears; if no ransom, the owner cuts off her nose
(1) a woman crushes one of a man's testicles in a quarrel; (2)* both testicles are damaged [no reproductive ability] [*The "two testicles" (2) portion of this ruling appears to be closest to the no-progeny concerns of Deut 25:11-12.]	(1) cut off one of her fingers (2)* gouge out both of her [breasts or eyes][a]

[12]The laws and palace decrees cited below are MAL A ¶¶ 4, 5, 8, 9, 15, 20, 24, 40, 44, 59 (cf. 57-58); MAL B ¶ 8; MAL F ¶¶ 1, 2; MAPD ¶¶ 2, 4-5, 17, 20, 21. See Roth, *Law Collections from Mesopotamia and Asia Minor*, pp. 153-209.

Crime	Punishment
a man touches a woman with sexual advances	cut off one of his fingers and, if he kissed her, cut off his lower lip with an ax blade
a man finds another man having sexual intercourse with his wife	he may kill them both, mutilate both—cut off his wife's nose; turn the man into a eunuch and have his face lacerated, or release both
a man sodomizes his comrade	sodomize the offending man and turn him into a eunuch
a wife leaves her husband and goes to live in another house with the support of the wife at this second residence	the one husband shall [mutilate] his abandoning wife; the other shall cut off the ears of his supportive wife
(1) a prostitute wears a veil in public or (2) a slave woman wears a veil in public	(1) strike the prostitute with 50 blows and pour hot tar over her head; (2) cut off the slave woman's ears
an owner's right to punish an Assyrian debt slave who lives in residence with him [unspecified offenses]	the owner [holder of the debt/ pledge] may whip the debt slave, pluck out the slave's hair, or mutilate or pierce the slave's ears
a husband's right to punish his wife [unspecified offenses]	a man may whip his wife, pluck out her hair, mutilate her ears and strike her [these four actions seem to be "in addition" to another list of punishments that may have included other mutilations][b]
incorporating a large piece of property from a neighbor's field	100 blows, repay triple the land wrongly taken, cut off one finger, one month in king's service
stealing sheep [crime not entirely clear in the text]	100 blows, replace stolen sheep, tear out person's hair, one month in king's service
a horse herder sells a horse without obtaining permission [and pockets the money?]	they shall lacerate his face

Crime	Punishment
an official reports a death within the king's household to the palace personnel without proper authorization	they shall cut off [his nose and ears?][c]
a palace woman gives gold, silver or precious stones to a palace slave	they shall cut off his [the slave's?] nose and ears
a palace woman makes an inappropriate curse	they shall pierce her nose and strike her with [blows of the rod]
a palace official allows an uncastrated court attendant to enter the palace	they shall amputate the court official's foot
a eunuch or court attendant eavesdrops on a palace woman	they shall cut off one of his ears

[a]Part of the MAL A ¶ 8 text is missing. However, a most likely reconstruction is that of gouging out either the woman's two breasts or her two eyes.

[b]The set of four punishments described in MAL A ¶ 59 are "in addition to" the ones written on the tablet, which may refer to the tablet and offenses mentioned immediately before (MALA ¶ ¶ 57-58). Unfortunately, these preceding texts are only partially legible. Nevertheless, it is important for our purposes to note that "cutting off" or mutilation is explicitly mentioned in this corrupted portion of text.

[c]The text is corrupted at this point. There is clearly a punishment of mutilation for the offence but its exact nature is uncertain.

Along similar lines, several Late Assyrian pieces of royal correspondence prescribe the penalty of pulling out or cutting out the tongue for lying to the king—a practice that is graphically portrayed in a stone relief from the reign of Ashurbanipal.[13]

Anatolian [Hittite] mutilation laws. The Anatolian region is located northwest of Israel in the area later known as Asia Minor or present-day Turkey. While Israel had less interaction with the Hittites than with Egypt, Babylon or Assyria, their legal codes from the Old Hittite period (c. 1650-1500 B.C.E.) and the Middle Hittite period (c. 1500-1180 B.C.E.) are nonetheless important because they are derived from roughly the same time frame as those we have already surveyed and hence provide helpful comparatives. Although most of their punishments are spelled out in terms of monetary compensation, the Hittite

---

[13]Tetlow, *Women, Crime, and Punishment in Ancient Law and Society*, pp. 165, 295 n. 170.

Crime	Punishment
a slave burglarizes a house	disfigure/mutilate the slave's nose and ears
a slave sets a house on fire	disfigure/mutilate the slave's nose and ears
slave committing theft	could be blinded[a]
sowing seed on top of another man's seed	two oxen teams pulled the offender's body in opposite directions [afterward both man and oxen were put to death][b]
soldier harmed the king	made blind and deaf [later the soldier was executed along with his family][c]
temple slave made his master angry	either (1) mutilate the nose, eyes, orears, or (2) death for offender along with death of his family[d]

[a]Tetlow (*Punishment in Ancient Law and Society*, p. 199) references such a blinding decree by a Middle Hittite king.

[b]This Old Hittite law combined a cruel form of corporal mutilation and death (Tetlow, *Punishment in Ancient Law and Society*, p. 186).

[c]James B. Pritchard, ed., "The Soldier's Oath" 3.1-10, *Ancient Near Eastern Texts Relating to the Old Testament*, 3rd ed. (Princeton, N.J.: Princeton University Press, 1969), pp. 353-54. Blinding seems to have been a standard punishment for any sort of traitor-type crime against the king. Cf. MH Letters 19 "From the King to Kassu," cited in Harry A. Hoffner Jr., *Letters from the Hittite Kingdom* (Atlanta: Society of Biblical Literature, 2009), pp. 119-21.

[d]Pritchard, "Instructions for Temple Officials" 2-3, 5-6, 8, 10, 14, 18-19, *Ancient Near Eastern Texts*, pp. 207-10.

law codes contain at least six cases of bodily mutilation.[14]

We could continue our ANE survey of corporal mutilation texts by looking at Persian law codes.[15] But since these texts come from an exilic and postexilic time period, they may be later than we wish to use in our ancient-world reconstruction. So I will end with this Hittite contribution. In any case, the portrait would not have changed much. The Persians continue with mutilation as a significant part of their legal codes and, in addition, become famous for some horrendous methods of torture and death. The scene is at least as grizzly if not worse. But we must

[14]HL ¶¶ 95, 99, 166. See Roth, *Law Collections from Mesopotamia and Asia Minor*, pp. 214-40.

[15]Pierre Briant, "Social and Legal Institutions in Achaemenid Iran [Persia]," in *Civilizations of the Ancient Near East*, ed. Jack M. Sasson (New York: Charles Scribner's, 1995), 1:524-26.

return to the hand-amputation passage of Deuteronomy 25 and reflect upon it within this broader historical setting.

A REDEMPTIVE-MOVEMENT UNDERSTANDING OF DEUTERONOMY 25:11-12

Reading through the ANE mutilation texts now permits us to see Deuteronomy 25:11-12 with a different set of eyes. While it is important not to lose sight of our contemporary context and what should almost certainly be considered a clear ethical improvement in penal codes (i.e., the abolishment of corporal mutilation altogether), it is equally important to start with viewing a text like Deuteronomy 25:11-12 through the lens of its ancient setting.

Redemptive-movement 1: Incredible ancient-world restraint. As we read the heavy knife text of Deuteronomy 25:11-12, the most striking component of redemptive movement has to be the comparative scarcity of mutilation laws within the Bible. Of course, I would be delighted if there were no amputation or mutilation texts at all. However, the fact that Deuteronomy 25:11-12 is the only prescribed corporal-mutilation punishment within the Bible is rather incredible given the ancient world in which it was written. In short, reading Scripture within its broader horizon helps us sense its monumental spirit of restraint. This restraint and greater dignity for human beings in punishment codes should be viewed as a partial step forward toward an ultimate ethical application (Z of fig. 2.1) that leaves a redemptive footprint of no small proportion.

Here is one way to sense the difference. In the five surrounding countries that we have observed (Sumer, Egypt, Babylon, Assyria and Anatolia) a combined total of roughly *fifty examples* of mutilation punishments were handed out for different crimes. The number is actually much larger than what the preceding survey includes (pushing closer to *one hundred examples*, in reality) since I have not included all mutilation cases. I have omitted from our survey a number of other ANE examples (1) with only a slight variation in crime, (2) with "open wounds" references connected to beatings, and (3) with clear statements about a body part being "cut off," but due to textual corruption, the exact nature of the mutilation and the crime itself are not sufficiently clear.[16] What should be obvious is the prevalence of mutilation within ANE codes compared with biblical law. Of course, if we approach Scripture and its singular mutilation text of Deuteronomy 25:11-12 from only our contemporary North American legal setting, which has abolished such amputation punishments altogether and views them as barbaric (rightly so, I think), then the picture is not a pretty one. We cannot get around the ugliness of the biblical portrait from the vantage point of our world. On the other hand, if we approach Scripture with an ancient, real-world expectation of finding somewhere between ten to twenty such mutilation texts within Scripture and, instead, find only one, then the picture changes. It is wonderfully redemptive. The biblical law codes show much greater restraint in this area. The biblical text is moving relative to its ancient-world context. For this sort of biblical phenomenon, at times I like to invoke a well-known line from *The Lion, the Witch, and the Wardrobe*, "Aslan is on the move." True, we have not completely changed seasons here. The change is not total in the sense of moving all the way from winter to summer. But the ice is starting to melt and the warmth of spring is coming. Ah, yes, one can sense our redemptive God at work.

Redemptive-movement 2: A better ancient-world alternative. Yet another way we encounter redemptive development within Scripture is through comparing the hand amputation text of Deuteronomy 25:11-12 with its closest parallel, namely, the "testicle grabbing" text within the Assyrian law codes. I have already argued that the best understanding of Deuteronomy 25:11-12 involves (1) the crime of a woman damaging a man's genitals to the extent that he is no longer able to procreate, and (2) the punishment of cutting off the woman's hand. The points of appropriate comparison with the parallel Assyr-

---

[16]These three areas of ancient mutilation examples (not included in this chapter's survey) are derived from (1) Egypt's perjury cases, (2) Egypt's frequent "open wounds" texts, and (3) several of Assyria's "cut off" texts, which are clearly amputation cases but too little of the surrounding context of the text survives to tell what the crime or punishment was. One of these Assyrian amputation texts may have originally included an entire list of acceptable amputations.

ian law would be (1) the similar crime of a woman damaging a man's genitals (both testicles, not just one testicle) to the point where he cannot have children, and (2) the very different mutilation punishment for the woman of either gouging out both of her eyes or cutting off both of her breasts.

Should this comparison be a valid one (see the interpretive elements developed earlier in this essay), then we are left with a comparison of three alternative punishments for roughly the same crime: the amputation of *one hand* (the Bible), the gouging out of *both eyes* (Assyrian option 1) or the cutting off of *both breasts* (Assyrian option 2). What I am going to suggest, as gruesome as the thought may sound, is that cutting off one hand is actually much less harsh than the two Assyrian options. First, if one considers losing both eyes, this comparative weighting can easily be made. Blindness in both eyes severely damages a person's capability of performing almost all daily tasks. The amputation of one hand, however, does not bring about anywhere near the same amount of damage or hardship. The primary disability of losing one hand is that of not being able to perform tasks that require two hands and particularly the grasping function that comes from one's fingers and palm. The loss of two-handed abilities is formidable to be sure. But the loss of both eyes is exponentially greater.

Second, a similar case can be made when we consider cutting off a hand compared with cutting off both breasts for a woman. Here it is important to understand the weighting of penal actions from the ancient-world setting within which they arise and not from our world. For instance, we must consider (1) the different values assigned to child bearing, and (2) the difference in need for maternal milk in the ANE context versus our context. The need for maternal milk in a premodern world was much greater without powdered alternatives and refrigeration. Also the inability to raise children in the ancient world was viewed as a huge economic threat to family stability and intergenerational care. Furthermore, the value of procreation was accentuated through the greater focus in the ancient setting on providing a lasting family name. While today, children bring a wonderful sense of procreative and family fulfillment, the component of name destiny and the economic benefits simply are not present as they used to be. Besides damage to her mothering capabilities, a woman losing both breasts would experience several other losses; it would diminish her marital attractiveness, the sexual arousal that come through the breasts, and a significant aspect of her gender identity.[17] Given these losses and accompanying values, most ancient women would probably have considered the amputation of both breasts as a far more devastating punishment than the cutting off of one hand.[18]

Due to the severity of all three punishments (one hand, two breasts or two eyes), this sort of value comparison is not something any of us really want to talk about let alone ponder what ancient women actually experienced by way of loss from such mutilations. However, when we reflect on the nature of the damages in each of the three cases, especially as they would have been understood and valued in the ANE world, the least harsh punishment by a significant measure is that of losing one hand. Once again, there is at least a certain degree of movement. And the movement is in the right direction—toward greater compassion and dignity in the midst of what is still, admittedly, an extremely harsh social environment.

Incremental movement with a redemptive spirit? Yes. Ultimate application? No. The redemptive spirit within the biblical text of Deuteronomy 25:11-12 may now be understood. We would never have been able to see this component of redemptive movement unless we had painstakingly read through and thought about the ancient-world context within which we find the hand amputation command of the Bible. Scripture as a whole moves away from the pervasive use of mutilation punishments that was part of its ancient world (only one example in the Bible compared to numerous in other ANE codes) and, even in the singular case of mutilation, it at least softens the punishment with a comparatively less-severe outcome.

Nevertheless, the biblical movement within a text like Deuteron-

---

[17]I might add the further (potential) loss of status for females within a polygamous household.

[18]The same comparative weighing (two breasts as more severe than one hand) may still be true for many women today. My point is that the difference between the two worlds leaves little doubt about which option would have been viewed as more harsh within the original context.

omy 25:11-12 must be considered at best as an incremental development of a biblical ethic along a continuum of crime-and-punishment
scenarios. The biblical text is headed toward something better. In no
way do the concrete specifics of what we encounter in Deuteronomy
25:11-12 represent an ultimate ethical application in terms of how to
treat human beings within a fallen-world context where punishments
are necessary. In other words, the contemporary abolishment of
bodily mutilation as punishment is a far better approach. This should
be obvious or intuitive. But let me explain briefly. Bodily mutilation
as a form of punishment is not the best or most helpful way of addressing wrongs between human beings. The reason is simple: *bodily
mutilation as a form of punishment provides only a destructive consequence with very little or no constructive or restorative aspect to the justice.* Instead, Christians should champion a much-improved ethic at
the concrete-specific level of meaning. Let the offending woman
keep her hand, her breasts and her eyes! Rather than destroying
something or someone, require the offender (to the extent possible)
to do something to undo the damages done. Create a penalty that
incorporates some element of corrective restitution and restoration
for the man she has damaged.[19] Punishments that can in some way
lessen or redeem damages are far better than punishments that create
more damage within an already damaged world.[20] They bring whole-

---

[19]So, what might a restorative consequence look like in the case of Deut 25:11-12? Rather than
chopping off a woman's hand (Deut 25:11-12), have her do something constructively to at least
in some measure undo the "lack of progeny" damages she has incurred. Within an ancient
world this might involve (1) some kind of levirate arrangement with the injured man's brother
to carry on the family name, (2) provide some other sort of surrogate childbirth through servants, or (3) pay something to offset the economic damages. In a present-day world we would
have to assess the motives and the circumstances (threat to the husband's life, size and strength
of the two men, etc.) and perhaps the genital injury might be viewed as reasonable force. However, even if some form of guilt and culpability were established for the rescuing wife, then
something like requiring payment toward IVF procedures (in vitro fertilization) might be an
appropriate step toward restorative justice.

[20]The resurgence of restorative justice today is good thing. However, its roots go back all the way
to the biblical notion of reparation or compensation with the *asham* sacrificial offering (often
translated "guilt" offering). Here worshipers are called on to do whatever they can to undo the
damages they have done. Instead of purely *destructive* penalties (i.e., merely making life more
difficult for offenders because of the hardship they have inflicted), a constructive penalty
makes much better sense and theologically accords well with the eschatological trajectory of
our faith. If at all possible, we should create a better world (not a more damaged world) through

ness to our fractured world. I will not belabor this point. But for me the core issue is an ethical one, which speaks loudly to why the hand amputation passage in terms of its concrete-specific teaching does not represent an ultimate ethical application. Such movement toward a Z-component of application (see fig. 2.1) comes only as we seek to carry further and be impacted to an even greater extent by Scripture's redemptive spirit.

For yet another reason the corporal punishment text of Deuteronomy 25:11-12 ought to be viewed as not achieving an ultimate ethical application within its concrete specificity. We might observe that this biblical case of bodily mutilation is directed toward a woman. Now skim back through the mutilation texts from the various ANE countries (Sumer, Egypt, Babylon, Assyria and Anatolia) and notice how many of them are directed toward those down the social ladder. Many of these harsh ANE mutilation texts are similarly aimed at the underlings within the power structures of the ancient society: children, women, slaves, prostitutes, hired workers, court attendants and the like. Those *up* the social ladder were far less apt to experience amputation as a punishment than those *down* the ladder. While the lopsided justice of Deuteronomy 25:11-12 is understandable given its ancient-world context, this lack of social and gender equality in biblical texts prompts us to reflect more broadly on the treatment of women in the Bible. This topic is not the focus of this book. Nevertheless, we might at least propose that a Christian ethic should carry the Bible's redemptive spirit forward with greater equality—it should champion the complete abolition of mutilation as a punitive action today and argue for alternative forms of justice that do not show partiality or inequity in relation to a person's social status.

THE CRUCIAL QUESTION: THE ROD, THE WHIP—AND THE HEAVY KNIFE?

Let's come back to this chapter's opening question. In view of the

---

the punishments that we enact.

clear teaching of the Bible, should Christians endorse a return to corporal punishment for adults? I responded to this question with a counterquestion: Are we willing to accept the whole range of corporal punishment within Scripture? After reading this chapter about the heavy knife and comparable ANE mutilation laws, the answer to this counterquestion ought to be a resounding no! We would be destined for a much less humane treatment of people in the area of punishment law should bodily mutilations from the Bible (or from any other source) ever be permitted again. There are plenty of alternative penalties and forms of punishment with far greater benefits and virtue.

Christians who entertain a return to adult corporal punishment because of instruction in the Bible must ponder whether they would be willing to endorse hand amputation today as taught in Deuteronomy 25. Even for those toying with a return to the rod and whip for adults, the idea of hand amputations is simply too repugnant. Most Christians cannot bring themselves to answer the question in the affirmative. If so, we must consider what a negative answer means for applying Scripture today. The implication for the ethics of punishment and the use of the Bible ought to be painfully obvious now. We cannot appeal to the biblical commands for a particular punishment as normative or as "ethically most redemptive" or as "an ultimate ethical application" for today simply because it is in the Bible. In the final analysis we cannot use the biblical teaching about corporal punishment for adults in order to validate the practice today. Whenever we are tempted to do so, some among us should stand up and cry out, "Remember the heavy knife!" We should also proclaim just as loudly, "Remember the seven ways we have journeyed beyond the rod and whip!" Of course, I am speaking of the seven ethical developments by Christians of a two-smacks-max pro-spanking persuasion (see chap. 1). In neither of these two "remember" cases is it likely that Christians would abandon their contemporary advanced or developed ethical position and return to cutting off a wife's hand (the heavy knife) or to using corporal punishment in seven ways that Scripture actually teaches in its concrete-specific instructions (the rod and the whip).

CONCLUSION

After reading this chapter no Christians, I hope, are inclined to ask for a return to adult corporal punishment within our contemporary justice system. To do so would be like Israel yearning for a return to Egypt after being set free from bondage. Returning to adult corporal punishment as taught within Scripture is a huge step backwards in terms of our present-day judicial practices.

Here is why. To the person who asks me about returning to adult corporal punishment I respond with two questions. Are you willing to return (1) to hand amputations with the knife or ax, and (2) to each of the seven ways (chap. 1) with the rod and whip? If a person is not prepared to go back on these ethical developments, and most Christians get a lump in their throat here (rightly so), then something follows from this reflection: ethical assessments must be made from a larger context of ethical discussion and linked to the redemptive spirit within these texts as we see that spirit lived out in better ways within our contemporary application. We cannot invoke the sanctity of any corporal punishment scenario (either bodily beatings or mutilations) simply because it is found in the Bible. Instead, our ethical reflection must embrace a logical and theological development of the redemptive spirit of these crime-and-punishment texts. Having said this, the logic of moving away from purely *destructive* punishments like the hand-amputation punishment of Deuteronomy 25:11-12 is that alternative *constructive* punishments can equally uphold social values but in a way that brings wholeness and healing, at least in part, to a broken world and especially to the damaged or injured person.

At this concluding point, let me now make explicit what my answer would be to the question of returning to adult corporal punishment—the use of the rod and whip today for adults. As developed at length in this chapter, the nature of our ethical critique about better punishments should be clear in the case of cutting off a woman's hand. What is true about "cutting off the hand" for adults is also true *on a lesser scale* for the rod and whip being used for adults today. There are better punishments than corporal punishment for adults—consequences that still inflict very real pain (due to various losses incurred) while having the positive benefit of constructively addressing the damages that the offender has inflicted on other human beings. This more constructive and restorative answer, not the return to corporal punishment for adults, makes for a better world—it frames our sense of justice within the core values of Christian theology, merges with the redemptive spirit within the troublesome texts (taking their redemptive spirit further in a contemporary context) and conveys our eschatological hope of a new world with complete redemption and wholeness.[21]

---

[21]The pitting of *corporal punishment* (rod/whip) against *jail time* for adults wrongly assumes that jail time is somehow the best option or only other option within our culture. This amounts to a false dichotomy and skewed perspective. Of course, many people would gladly take a certain amount of beatings (per year) to reduce their jail time. But, neither of these two options (the beatings option or the jail-time option) do much to create a better, less-damaged world. I would advocate for (1) jail time with meaningful work camps, where the person's income goes toward helping those he or she has damaged or (2) a governmental garnishee of 10 percent of wages outside of prison in order to help repay damages. This restorative focus would place the offender in the required role of making amends through positive actions. These are only two sample examples; the real-life options are endless.

5

WHAT ABOUT USING ONLY
NONCORPORAL METHODS
FOR CHILDREN?

This chapter addresses the classic parenting question, Should I spank my kids? From a hermeneutical vantage point, the question might better be asked this way: *Having already journeyed beyond the concrete-specific teaching of the Bible about "beatings with the rod" (the seven ways) to a gentler and kinder form of discipline (two-smacks-max)—a journey that embraces the redemptive spirit of Scripture—should that same redemptive spirit logically carry Christians to use alternative-discipline methods only?* In other words, can Christians take the redemptive-movement meaning in Scripture to a greater level of fulfillment or toward a more developed ethical application of the Bible that pushes beyond two-smacks-max?

Two-smacks-max proponents of course use various forms of alternative noncorporal methods of discipline alongside their spanking practices. The word *only* in "alternative-discipline methods *only*" makes this clear. Therefore, the question of this chapter could also be put this way: Should Christians remove two-smacks-max spanking from their parenting mix and use *only* noncorporal methods of discipline? In short, should Christians today adopt *two-smacks-max* or *alternative-discipline methods only?*

PERSPECTIVE ON THE QUESTION

My objective is *not* to widen the gap between pro-spankers and alternative-methods parenting groups. Rather, I hope to bring these two Christian groups closer together. Parents and scholars on both sides of the spanking issue need to see that ethical movement within the Christian community goes beyond the concrete-specific teaching of Scripture about corporal punishment and thus—ironically—both contemporary groups are much closer in what they share than in what separates them. For this reason, despite our differences, I can genuinely express gratitude for James Dobson, for Focus on the Family ministries and for Jim Daly (the new president of Focus on the Family). When we understand how both two-smacks-max people and alternative-discipline-only folk have journeyed together in their ethical application of the Bible, we need to celebrate the overlapping commonality. What we share is far greater than any differences.

If we employ a sports analogy, we might say that the discussion in this chapter concerns the last mile of a marathon. The degree and magnitude of ethical development on this issue is nearly complete for *both* groups—(1) the pro-spankers of the two-smacks-max sort, who embrace the seven ways of ethical development, and (2) the alternative-discipline-only people who use effective noncorporal methods of child discipline. The finish line for the *ultimate ethical application of Scripture* (see Z in fig. 2.1) is almost in view for both groups. We have run together for the majority of the marathon distance; now we are looking toward its end. We are trying to envision the finish line. Our exploration in this chapter, then, is about how to see those last few staggering steps—that last mile of the race. In so doing, let's not forget that we are coparticipants in what is by far most of the marathon's distance.

Having painted a "more commonality than differences" perspective, I will now advance a twofold thesis. First, this chapter argues that Christians are under *no obligation* in terms of biblical authority to continue using corporal punishment even in the highly modified form of two-smacks-max. Christians are free to use only alternative, noncorporal methods in their childrearing practices with God's blessing on their lives. Second, at least in a modest or moderate sense Christians are under a *moral obligation* to take the redemptive spirit already within Scripture to a greater fulfillment than what has been realized by two-smacks-max proponents. I do not want to overstate the case—the ethical commonality is far greater than our differences. Nevertheless, effective noncorporal methods of discipline (alternative-discipline-only) provide a comparatively better way yet (beyond two-smacks-max) in which Christian parents can journey toward an ultimate ethical application of Scripture (Z in fig. 2.1).

NO OBLIGATION FOR CHRISTIANS TO STAY WITH TWO-SMACKS-MAX

For at least two reasons Christian parents are under no obligation to stay with two-smacks-max practices. Should they choose to leave corporal punishment altogether (even in the form of two-smacks-max), this is completely acceptable within the bounds of biblical authority. Christians who practice discipline with only noncorporal means can still fulfill the parenting requirements of Scripture.

The abstracted and purpose meaning of Scripture. If parents want to abandon two-smacks-max methods of child discipline and move to alternative-discipline-only approaches, they should not fear God's disapproval. As with our discussion of the garage-cleaning story (chap. 3), the son who uses a shop vacuum to clean out the garage after being handed a broom hardly deserves a parental scolding. Rather, he deserves praise. Similarly, through the use of alternative, noncorporal means, parents can be faithful to the instructions about "beating your child with a rod" as long as they fulfill the abstracted meaning of discipline your children.[1] (See the postscript for numerous noncorporal methods of discipline, some of which are far more powerful and effective than two-smacks-max.) If parents obey the abstracted instruction of Scripture to "discipline their children" and do so by using a metaphorical rod of noncorporal discipline, then their choices have God's approval.

Furthermore, Christian parents who use alternative-discipline-only approaches in raising their children can easily fulfill the purpose mean-

---

[1]Commentators on Proverbs often emphasize that "discipline" is the important component of meaning in the rod proverbs, and not the form of discipline (see Paul E. Koptak, *Proverbs*, NIVAC [Grand Rapids: Zondervan, 2003], p. 362).

ing of the rod-and-whip texts. The teaching of Proverbs is clearly that the rod and whip will help *drive out folly and encourage wisdom*—the negative and positive purposes of corporal punishment for both children and adults. If parents achieve these dual purposes through using the metaphorical, noncorporal rod of alternative-discipline-only practices, then once again their actions rest under the smile and approval of God. They have fulfilled what it genuinely means to be under the authority of Scripture.

Given this consideration about scriptural meaning, we have to wonder why two-smacks-max proponents hold so tightly to their spanking practices. Many pro-spankers think that a departure from spanking erodes the authority of the Bible. But nothing could be further from the truth if we consider Scripture's abstracted meaning (discipline) and purpose meaning (avoid folly and pursue wisdom), as it was developed in earlier chapters. Achieving these two aspects of biblical meaning through alternative-discipline-only methods of child discipline brings God's affirmation and favor. Is there something *sacred* about the broom for cleaning out the garage? Not likely. The functional aspect of biblical commands is far more important than form. The functional component (discipline, turning from folly and embracing wisdom) is sacred, not the instrument or means. Consequently, Christians are free—absolutely free—to pursue alternative methods or means.

The New Testament should not hold us back. Someone might object to the redemptive-trajectory thesis developed within this chapter (calling parents to embrace alternative-discipline-only practices) since it is nowhere explicitly taught within the New Testament. I would agree with this observation. We do not find any statement within the New Testament that calls for Christians to abolish corporal punishment of children and use alternative means of discipline only. Pro-spankers might argue that since (1) the New Testament seems to uphold Old Testament patterns of discipline (Heb 12:5-11), and (2) the New Testament lacks any explicit denouncement of corporal punishment, a Christian must not abandon the two-smacks-max method. We could add a third and fourth consideration, namely, that (3) Christians within the early church practiced corporal punishment, and (4) Jesus himself refers to corporal beatings in a seemingly positive, or at least nonderogatory, fashion as he described eschatological judgment (Lk 12:47-48).[2]

However, the idea that the New Testament solidifies the sanctity of corporal punishment for children forgets two important lessons. First, an appeal to the New Testament to endorse two-smacks-max practices for children forgets a crucial lesson from the *adult* rod-and-whip texts. Scripture clearly teaches the use of the rod and whip for adults. Proverbs uses the same functional ideas about driving out foolishness and embracing wisdom as the purpose behind adult beatings (the same good purposes as with beating children). Furthermore, the previous points about the New Testament—upholding Old Testament patterns, no explicit denouncements, early Christian practice and even Jesus' statements—could equally be used to support *adult* beatings with the rod and whip. Again, should we be tempted to resume using adult corporal punishment, please reread chapter four and ponder why the rod, the whip and the heavy knife ought to be rejected by contemporary Christians. If the reasoning from chapter four is valid, then the church today is *already living out a redemptive-movement thesis* regarding adult corporal punishment with conclusions that move far beyond the concrete particulars of the New Testament. True enough—there are no explicit denouncements of adult corporal punishment in the New Testament. But that silence does not outweigh other considerations. Alternative methods of helping adults find wisdom and avoid folly are readily available today that are much better than beatings with the rod and whip; these alternative methods honor Scripture's redemptive spirit by moving forward with it.

Second, any appeal to the New Testament to validate two-smacks-max practices forgets the lesson that the church has learned from the slavery texts. Like the corporal punishment discussions, pro-slavery proponents held that the New Testament endorses slavery through theological analogy (God is master; all Christians are slaves metaphor-

---

[2]Jesus most likely used a whip to drive out the larger livestock (not humans) within the temple scene of John 2:13-22 (see N. Clayton Croy, "The Messianic Whippersnapper: Did Jesus Use a Whip on People in the Temple (John 2:15)?" *Journal of Biblical Literature* 128, no. 3 [2009]: 555-68). Therefore, this text is not a suitable support for the beating of people.

ically), the continued practice of slavery by New Testament Christians, the New Testament upholding Old Testament ownership of slaves, Jesus' teaching about eschatological punishment with a nonderogatory illustration about the beating of slaves (Lk 12:47-48), and the fact that the New Testament nowhere explicitly teaches the abolition of slavery.

Pro-slavery Christians did not want to venture beyond the Bible in any sense. Rather, they wanted to stay with the concrete specificity of the biblical text, as outlined in both Testaments, because it offered a sense of safety. Listen to the words of the nineteenth-century author John Henry Hopkins (1792-1868), who could not bring himself to accept an abolitionist viewpoint on slavery.

> If it were a matter to be determined by personal sympathies, tastes, or feelings, I should be as ready as any man to condemn the institution of slavery, for all my prejudices of education, habit, and social position stand entirely opposed to it. But as a Christian . . . I am compelled to submit my weak and erring intellect to the authority of the Almighty. For then only can I be *safe* in my conclusions.[3]

Like Hopkins, many Christians today look for safety and certainty in their interpretive conclusions. They feel that if they root their conclusions for a contemporary ethic within a concrete, on-the-page understanding, such a move has the approval of God and thus provides the safety they are looking for. Yet maybe Scripture was not written in order to establish a utopian society with complete justice and equity in the immediacy of its original setting. I suspect it is *we* who are impatient; we want a fully packaged ethic with all of its glorious details at the drop of a hat. Instead, Scripture gives us an ethic that needs in some ways to be developed and worked out over time. It would appear that a number of biblical texts were written with limited or *incremental movement* toward an ultimate ethical application. If so, then movement meaning within the text itself ought to tug at our heartstrings and beckon us to go further. We must be willing to take this journey even if, as in the case of the slavery texts, it carries us well beyond the

---

[3]John Henry Hopkins, quoted in J. Albert Harrill, *Slaves in the New Testament: Literary, Social and Moral Dimensions* (Minneapolis: Augsburg Fortress, 2006), p. vii (italics added).

concrete-specific instructions of the New Testament.[4]

True safety cannot be found in blindly following the concrete instructions of the Bible and in stopping with a frozen-in-time, incrementally developed ethic seen in the New Testament slavery texts. It would be a shame if we did this for fear that we might offend God. True safety means rooting our Christian ethic in the redemptive spirit of the biblical text so that through logical and theological extension we can explore ways of moving toward an ultimate application of Scripture. Therein we enjoy God's blessing.

In sum, Christians are under no obligation to stay with two-smacks-max methods of disciplining children today. Given that noncorporal methods can equally fulfill Scripture's abstracted and purpose meaning, Christians are free to embrace an alternative-discipline-only option as an acceptable way of living out biblical authority. Those who think that departing from two-smacks-max undermines the Bible are misguided at best. Furthermore, to claim that the New Testament prevents Christians from abandoning two-smacks-max and from taking up an alternative-discipline-only approach invokes a faulty hermeneutical framework. We must learn the lessons of the past—living out the redemptive spirit of Scripture means that we are inspired by its redemptive heartbeat, and we must not be constrained by the partially realized ethic within its concrete instructions. The hermeneutical lessons from the slavery texts and from the adult corporal punishment texts confirm that Christians are indeed free to pursue an alternative-discipline-only option in the discipline of children.

Now we must press on with another question. So far this chapter has argued that Christians are *free* to embrace an alternative-discipline-only option. The next question to ask is whether Christians *ought* to embrace an alternative-discipline-only parenting approach. Is there any moral obligation for Christians to go further than two-smacks-max? Should

---

[4]Only a few scholars would argue that the New Testament teaches abolitionism within its concrete-specific instructions. While we might wish for this to be the case, attempts to demonstrate that it does unfortunately present a distorted understanding of the New Testament slavery passages (see William J. Webb, "A Response to Walter C. Kaiser Jr.," in *Four Views on Moving Beyond the Bible to Theology*, ed. Gary T. Meadors [Grand Rapids: Zondervan, 2009], pp. 64-70).

we travel further in this redemptive journey? The rest of this chapter outlines a case for why abandoning two-smacks-max and embracing alternative-discipline-only methods in the treatment of children takes the redemptive spirit of Scripture to an even greater fulfillment.

AN OBLIGATION TO TAKE THE REDEMPTIVE SPIRIT FURTHER

This book has argued for reading the corporal punishment texts—the rod, the whip and the heavy knife—within their ancient historical context. Only from the horizon of an ancient Near Eastern world can a reader understand these troubling texts in a different light—one that encounters their redemptive-movement meaning. The forty lashes of Deuteronomy 25:1-3 must be understood against its ancient social context, which included beatings of up to two hundred lashes or strokes, open wounds, bodily mutilations and other forms of torture-like punishment (see chap. 3). The hand amputation text of Deuteronomy 25:11-12 (the only case of prescribed mutilation within the Bible) is actually less harsh than its Assyrian counterpart, and Scripture as a whole evidences considerable restraint within—and redemptive movement away from—an ancient world where one might have expected ten to twenty such mutilation prescriptions (see chap. 4). Similarly, the slave-beating texts of Exodus 21:20-21, 26-27 as we read them within their ANE context show dramatic movement toward greater protection and dignity of the slave.[5] These texts illustrate that an important component of meaning within the corporal punishment texts is their redemptive movement. The essence of this *redemptive-movement meaning* may be framed as follows:

- less harsh, softer forms of punishment

- movement toward greater kindness and gentleness

- increased protection and safety of the person being beaten

- explicit emphasis on the honor and dignity of the person being punished

---

[5]See the discussion of these Exodus texts in chap. 2.

- much greater restraint compared to ANE brutality

- *summary:* a better treatment of human beings in punishment or disciplinary scenarios

The remainder of this chapter will make a case for why a logical extension or trajectory of the redemptive spirit of Scripture should lead Christians to abolish corporal beatings and mutilations altogether. We need to journey beyond even the highly improved two-smacks-max and move courageously toward noncorporal alternative-discipline-only expressions of discipline.

An analogy: The abolition of slavery, not just nicer slavery. By way of analogy, the Christian argument for the abolition of slavery casts light on how to apply the redemptive-movement meaning within the corporal punishment texts. When the slavery texts are read within their ANE environment, they provide wonderful elements of redemptive movement toward a better treatment of fellow humans (see chap. 2). The slavery texts evidence a broad redemptive trend toward something considerably better—greater kindness, gentleness, dignity and worth. It is the logical extension of this redemptive spirit that carries us to the abolition of slavery altogether.

An ultimate ethical application of Scripture's redemptive spirit (Z in fig. 2.1) within the slavery texts calls for the abolition of slavery and replacing it with a better form—the freedom of all human beings. Sometimes a particular form needs abolishing and replacing with something better. It simply would not do for the church to endorse a kinder and gentler form of slavery—and to keep doing so in incremental measures of improvement. The greatest expression of kindness and human dignity meant the abolition of slavery completely, not simply a "nicer" form of slavery. In a similar way, a logical extension or trajectory of the redemptive spirit within the corporal punishment texts means the abolition of physical beatings and bodily mutilations altogether. Softer and gentler beatings are good but do not offer the fullest expression of redemptive movement. Less harsh mutilations (a finger instead of a hand) are better than harsher forms, but obviously not an ultimate ethical application of Scripture's redemptive spirit.

In what remains, I develop five arguments for why abolishing physical beatings altogether (even in the two-smacks-max form) and embracing alternative-discipline-only advances a fulfillment of the redemptive spirit within the corporal punishment texts. Ethical reflection that overlaps or intersects with the redemptive-movement meaning in the Bible helps us see how and where we can take our application of Scripture's redemptive spirit to an even greater level.

More gentle (less harsh) means. As mentioned earlier, redemptive movement within the corporal punishment texts means moving toward a gentler or less harsh treatment of human beings. For the most part Scripture moves away from extremely cruel and inhumane forms of punishment within an ANE world—such is its redemptive spirit. Along these lines I have commended two-smacks-max proponents for their departure from the concrete instructions of the Bible and their marked advancements in this area. Their departure represents biblical obedience (not disobedience) in the truest sense because they have taken Scripture's redemptive-movement meaning to yet another level. But we might still ask: can that spirit of gentleness and less-harsh punishments be taken even further by moving beyond two-smacks-max? In the ethical reflection that follows we need to think about the related, flipside issue of cruelty and violence within our present-day setting. I argue that our ethical obligation for the least (or no) violent means if possible is a very relevant expression of the biblical concern for less harsh and more gentle means of punishment or behavioral correction.

Before tackling the subject of the least (or no) violent means possible, let's untangle some of the confusion surrounding the idea of hitting today. One classic argument against spanking is that it raises a contradiction about hitting people. The argument goes like this. Parents teach children, by their example, that it is okay for a parent (a big person) to hit them and cause physical pain. In the next breath a child is instructed to go and play with friends, and they are told not hit other kids. Perhaps this contradiction is most intensely felt when the parent hits the child as an act of discipline after the child has (wrongly) hit a brother or sister.

While I grant a seeming contradiction, this antispanking argument is not a good one. I would suggest that the contradiction is more apparent than real. There is (or should be) a huge difference in the intention and motives between the one case of hitting and the other. Thus the hitting-contradiction argument, at least in its present surface-level formulation, does not persuade me to change my mind. Most of us would agree that some limited violence is needed at times, regrettably, in order to maintain order in a fallen society. All of us recognize the need for a police force that must use various forms of violence for good restraining purposes. So the surface contradiction about hitting should not persuade anyone to move away from spanking with the two-smacks-max method.

Nevertheless, a second level to the hitting argument has considerable merit. The only way that pro-spankers can defend the actions of parents hitting a child is by appealing (rightly so) to the use of limited violence for restraining purposes, as would be the case with the police force. Yet once this counterargument is made, it pushes us into a new sort of second-level dialogue. It necessitates further reflection about the use of limited or restrained violence. In general we all recognize that the ethics of limited violence calls for using such regrettable force (1) only to the extent required, and (2) only if absolutely necessary. This twofold restriction is important. Remember, the police are ethically bound to use the lowest level of violent intervention needed to achieve their proper goals. They cannot use *any* violent actions (none at all) unless that is the *only* way to achieve their goals. In other words, police officers are morally constrained to use only forms of nonviolent intervention if that will do the job.

What this means for parents is that we have a moral obligation (like the police force) to use nonviolent means of intervention with our children *if that will get the job done*. Such a commitment to no violence or hitting if possible intersects with the redemptive-movement meaning within the corporal punishment texts of the Bible. It is another way of talking about the Bible's movement of people toward kinder and gentler (less harsh or cruel) forms of punishment. What should strike us as cruel or harsh in evaluating police actions is the use of *more* violent means than necessary, such as (1) the police using guns with real bullets when only clubs and mace are needed, (2) the use of clubs with excessive beatings when only a shield barrier and tear gas are needed, or (3) the use of any hitting when only nonphysical corrective measures are needed.

No parent should use even limited violence of hitting a child once or twice (two-smacks-max) in order to correct behavior or offset greater harm if they can achieve the same disciplinary goals through other nonviolent means.[6] Like an ethically restrained law enforcement officer, Christians parents have a moral obligation if at all possible (and it is quite possible) to achieve good disciplinary goals through nonviolent means. This ethical reflection converges with our need to fulfill the redemptive spirit of Scripture and find forms of discipline or punishment for children that embody a greater expression of its movement toward kinder and gentler (less harsh) means.

Greater protection and less potential for abuse. Redemptive movement within the slave-beating texts (as read within an ANE world) speaks loudly about the concern for the physical protection and safety of the slave (see chap. 2). Such a redemptive component within the Bible ought to influence our thinking today when we consider the matter of abuse. While two-smacks-max has made tremendous progress to offset the likelihood of physical abuse, we might ask if further movement with respect to physical protection and safety can be achieved. A logical extension of the biblical spirit in this area of physical protection should cause parents to err on the side of greater safety, not greater risk.

I wish to separate myself from extremist antispankers who shout "abuse" at all uses of corporal punishment with children. This amounts to a one-size-fits-all fallacy in the critique of corporal punishment methods today. It indiscriminately lumps together parents who beat their kids black and blue in a fit of rage, using an object designed to inflict pain, with parents who lovingly and calmly give their kids a smack or two (max) on the behind with their open palm in order to

---

[6]This "no violence if at all possible" argument slowly worked on my mind over the years as I began to understand its congruence with Scripture. I gradually softened in my spanking convictions due to this ethical reflection. It caused me as a parent to start giving alternative noncorporal disciplinary methods a greater chance in our home. I discovered that child discipline was in fact quite possible through effective noncorporal means (no hitting).

provide something of a ritualized no in their teaching discourse. So it seems highly inappropriate and indiscriminate to label the two-smacks-max approach as abusive.

Rather, I would argue that the two-smacks-max method has a greater *potential* for abuse than noncorporal methods of child discipline. When a parent is exhausted and living on emotional fumes (something that will inevitably happen to every parent from time to time), it is not hard to feel extremely angry about the misbehavior of a child. It is at this flashpoint that the method has the greatest potential for abuse. This is not really a difficulty intrinsic to the method itself. The difficulty is in using such a method within a fallen world with imperfect parents who are doing the disciplinary procedures. Any time an adult mixes hitting a child (even using the highly restrained two-smacks-max approach) with the volatile factor of parental anger or wrongly estimated strength, then in the heat of the moment the potential arises to overdo it—in order words, abuse.

Admittedly, any method of parenting can be accompanied by abuse. Alternative noncorporal methods of discipline are also open to abuse. I am not suggesting that any one method is failsafe in this area. Nevertheless, alternative-discipline-only methods cause a parent to focus on a *thinking* way and not a *hitting* way of addressing the behavioral problem. When a parent has to employ a thinking solution to behavior issues, it slows down the process of discipline in a good way.

The moral obligation here in moving from two-smacks-max to alternative-discipline-only methods might be compared to the purchase of high quality winter tires like Bridgestone Blizzaks or Michelin X-Ice tires. Yes, a good driver can use all-season tires on a vehicle and drive in a reasonably safe manner throughout the winter season. But proper snow tires add to the margin of safety by significantly reducing the risk of losing control of the vehicle when driving on snow or ice. In a similar fashion, if alternative-discipline-only methods can get the discipline job done (see the postscript for effective methods), then why would parents not want to select this course of greater safety? Taking preventative action to decrease the likelihood of damage to ourselves and others is not a morally neutral concept. Parents have at least a moderate ethical obligation here. Most importantly, such a positive action aligns well with of the redemptive movement within Scripture to advance the safety and protection of the person being punished.

More constructive means. Chapter four (on Deut 25:11-12) surveyed numerous ANE mutilation texts, several of which even prescribed mutilating children as an act of discipline. When reading the corporal punishment texts of the Bible within this mutilation-obsessed world, one thing is quite clear about the redemptive movement within Scripture compared to its ancient social context: Scripture is headed toward more constructive (less destructive) means of punishment. Its steps are incremental. But they are real, and we need to capture their spirit as we reflect on actions of punishment today. Similar to moving away from the heavy knife and adult beatings with the rod, one must consider with all punishment scenarios (even with two-smacks-max) the degree to which the punishment is constructive in nature.

A distinct advantage of alternative-discipline-only methods is that Christians can explore a whole series of more constructive means to discipline. This may sound confusing to two-smacks-max proponents who think that what they do with children *is* constructive. After all, by hitting children once or twice, they are helping children embrace good behavior and live wisely. Yes, this is constructive. But it is constructive in terms of the outcome or ends or purpose. We have previously discussed how good ends do not justify the means (chap. 3), and how more constructive means in adult corporal punishment, for example, represent a greater fulfillment of Scripture's redemptive spirit (chap. 4). So the point here is about constructive *means* to an end and not about the constructive ends.

If we can frame more constructive means to achieve the same good ends, then ethical advancement has been made. Since this more constructive means argument has been the focus of the last chapter within adult punishment scenarios, we need only to transfer the same logic into the sphere of children. There exist today more constructive means of disciplining children than by hitting them. Joining together (1) a *more* constructive means with (2) the *same* good constructive ends or outcomes provides a better ethical combination. It allows us to carry the redemptive spirit of Scripture further.

Greater dignity and honor. Scripture's movement away from harsh ANE punishments and toward gentler forms was due to a concern for the dignity and honor of the one being punished. The redemptive movement itself infers such a value, but the text of Deuteronomy 25:3 makes it explicit. If we consider a logical extension of this redemptive spirit within the Bible, it should lead us to forms of discipline that uphold the best expression of human dignity and honor possible. While many Christians may not have pondered the issue of dignity and honor when it comes to child discipline, it is well worth the reflection. A concern for a greater sense of human dignity and honor ultimately leads us beyond two-smacks-max and toward the alternative-discipline-only approach.

Think for a moment about adults who lack reasoning capabilities. In situations involving discipline or behavioral correction Christians ought to value the greatest possible dignity and honor for all persons (not just children) who lack adult reasoning capabilities. Probably the best way to truly grasp this dignity and honor argument and to have its ethical constraints tug at your heart is to imagine an *adult* (young or old) or even a teenager you know who is mentally challenged. The person could be from thirteen to over one hundred years old; the age does not really matter. Rather, what matters is that this person functions with a mental capacity like that of a preschooler, without the capability of adult reasoning. Due to diminished brain capacity, your attempts at reasoning only accelerate conflict and anxiety in this person; it does not bring about behavioral change and resolution.

Here is the ethical reflection. With the actual face of this mentally challenged person in mind, picture yourself using corporal punishment as a means of behavioral correction. Can you imagine hitting him or her with a physical instrument or with your hand in order to effect behavioral change? I suspect not. If you ponder the reason why such an action would be difficult, if not impossible, it likely boils down to a sense of their human dignity. Hitting an adult who cannot reason violates the very core of who he or she is as a person, even if such hitting may effect behavioral change. Can you imagine hitting teenagers in a group home where the residents are mentally challenged and lack adult reasoning capabilities? Or can you contemplate hitting elderly people with dementia or Alzheimer's disease, or hitting a young adult with Down syndrome who lives with a developmental disability that impairs their cognition, or hitting *any* person who reasons in a less-than-typical-adult or even childlike way?

If you come to a no-hitting conclusion about teens or adults who lack advanced reasoning capability, it tends to dismantle a two-smacks-max position. Here is why. The two-smacks-max position is built on the premise that spanking must be maintained for children because they cannot reason as adults. Conversely, two-smacks-max proponents argue that older children and teens no longer require spanking because of their developed reasoning capabilities (see citations in chap. 1). But if this is so, then Christians must concede a need for the continued use of corporal punishment for teens and adults with diminished mental capacity. Yet we do not (and cannot bring ourselves to) hit adults who lack adult reasoning capabilities because we have come to view such actions as a gross violation of their human dignity.

So what about the human dignity of children? Are children *full* human beings even at a very young age? Of course they are. I am not talking about treating children with indulgence. That is a sick, twisted and insidious part our culture. But if we are talking about human dignity—the same human dignity accorded to adults even if they lack reasoning capabilities, then this is quite another matter. If hitting adults who lack logical cognitive capabilities assaults our sense of human dignity, then why do we continue to hit children? The answer is that we have wrongly accepted a view of children that accords them less human dignity than adults with no reasoning capability.[7]

This is not an easy argument to grasp. I have had to learn the authenticity of this argument through a painful lesson about human dignity and honor from my oldest son (now twenty-four), who has a degenerative brain disease. (The postscript tells his story and how our

---

[7]Of course, there should be greater honor shown to elderly people (a biblical virtue) by those who are younger. But that is not what I am talking about here. Nor does this sort of greater-age deference detract from the basic human dignity we should grant to all adult human beings, regardless of age.

experience with him, among other considerations, helped us change our minds about how to discipline.) Regardless of how we come to wrestle with this argument, the alternative-discipline-only option has the redemptive-movement advantage of advancing the human dignity of children in the same way that a noncorporal approach does for adults who have little or no reasoning capacity. The lack of reasoning ability does not diminish the need for behavioral correctives. But this behavioral change can be accomplished with alternative-discipline-only practices for both childlike adults and young children with a stronger expression of human dignity and honor. In turn, we do a better job of fulfilling Scripture's redemptive-movement meaning.

Christian witness in our world. Christians ought to consider how their parenting actions affect their witness for Jesus in an unbelieving world. Of course, wild and out-of-control children are not a good testimony to God's redeeming grace and kingdom reign in our world. But if parents can help grow well-behaved children who show respect for people and property through solid noncorporal methods of discipline, the question about Christian witness is one we ought to ponder.

Many Christians are beginning to wrestle with the witnessing implications that flow out of their parenting actions. Those who still use two-smacks-max are often not consistent between what they do in public versus what they do in private. In our North American context, hitting children in public (even using the restrained two-smacks-max method) will not go over well with many observers. At the very least, parents who use corporal punishment in public risk significant disdain from those who label all forms of corporal punishment as abusive.

If at all possible, followers of Jesus want to live before their neighbors in such a manner that these neighbors find the gospel attractive. Should your neighbors perceive spanking as morally objectionable (and especially if the redemptive movement and ethical discussion in this chapter has some merit), you might want to consider whether two-smacks-max is really the Christian flag that you want to fly on your front lawn. Provided we can still effectively discipline our kids through noncorporal methods, the alternative-discipline-only approach is the direction to go for the sake of our Christian witness.

The question about Christian witness is doubly problematic in our contemporary world when it comes to the corporal punishment texts of the Bible. Many non-Christians are aware of the troubling aspects of the corporal punishment texts—the ethically problematic rod-and-whip texts and the heavy-knife amputation text. The new atheism movement and its high-profile representatives like Richard Dawkins have made it their business to discredit Christians through casting high-beam spotlights on certain unsightly passages in the Bible.[8] We must introduce non-Christians to a redemptive-movement under-standing of the biblical text and help them read the corporal punish-ment texts through an ancient-world lens. Such a witnessing act gives them a greater opportunity to believe that God may have in fact had something to do with the writing of Scripture. But our apologetic must go deeper. We must do more than simply help them to *read* Scripture differently. We must *live out* what we believe about Scrip-ture's redemptive spirit. Non-Christians must see that the redemptive movement within the Bible itself continues to affect our lives. They must see us striving for an ultimate ethical application of Scripture in the practical ways that we engage our children and address their need for discipline and correctives.

If how we *act* toward children in our parenting practices and what we *say* about the troubling corporal punishment texts intersect in a con-firming and consistent redemptive fashion, then followers of Jesus might actually be able to engage their neighbors in a positive and pro-active way. We should not cling to ancient forms of discipline that are ethically problematic when effective noncorporal methods are available that allow us to achieve the good purposes of Scripture, namely, help-ing children avoid folly and learn wisdom. The obligation to live out better discipline methods and to tell non-Christians about a better way

---

[8]See Richard Dawkins, *The God Delusion* (Boston: Mariner, 2006), pp. 268-316; Christopher Hitchens, *God Is Not Great: How Religion Poisons Everything* (Toronto: McClelland & Stewart, 2007), pp. 97-122. Cf. John Shelby Spong, *The Sins of Scripture* (New York: HarperCollins, 2005), pp. 143-60 (section on beating children); Charles Kimball, *When Religion Becomes Evil* (New York: HarperCollins, 2003). For a recent evangelical response that uses a redemptive-movement hermeneutic (among other strategies) within an apologetic framework, see Paul Copan, *Is God a Moral Monster? Making Sense of the Old Testament God* (Grand Rapids: Baker, 2011).

to understand Scripture is part of our Christian witness; it is a dual witness that is not optional for the followers of Jesus.

CONCLUSION

The spanking question is an important one. Should Christians choose two-smacks-max or alternative-discipline-only methods for disciplining their children? Given that effective noncorporal methods of discipline can achieve good behavior with children (see the postscript), this chapter has argued that Christians are under *no moral obligation* to stay with two-smacks-max practices. They are free to embrace alternative-discipline-only parenting methods.

But there is more. Scripture's redemptive movement warrants taking this "free to move" conclusion one step further. Christians are not only free to move; they should move to alternative-discipline-only methods. For a number of reasons presented here *Christians are under a moral obligation* to leave behind two-smacks-max and embrace an alternative-discipline-only option. Yes, this choice is moderate compared with the seven ways that movement has already taken place. Nevertheless, alternative-discipline-only discipline carries the redemptive spirit and ethical application of Scripture further in five important ways: more gentle (least violent) means, increased safety against abuse, more constructive means, greater human dignity, and enhanced Christian witness. Like the changes adopted within the seven ways of the two-smacks-max position, embracing an alternative-discipline-only approach to parenting is not a mere swapping out of equivalents. It represents a real and significant ethical development based on redemptive-movement meaning within the corporal punishment texts themselves.

CONCLUSION

DARE TO READ THE BIBLE DIFFERENTLY

The primary focus of this book has been on hermeneutics—how we read and apply our Bibles. The corporal punishment texts have provided a fascinating window through which Christians can look at how we embrace biblical teaching about the rod, whip and heavy knife. In short, God's redemptive spirit as well as the movement meaning within the biblical text must carry us forward to an ultimate ethical application of Scripture. True biblical authority does not mean replicating the concrete-specific instructions of the Bible, but holding fast to the redemptive spirit within the biblical text and finding contemporary expressions that truly carry its original-setting ethical development to a yet greater level of fulfillment.

A redemptive-movement approach is neither a new nor a stand-alone hermeneutic. A redemptive-movement understanding of the Bible is merely a component within a standard grammatical-historical hermeneutic. As Christians we often do well in discovering meaning by reading texts within their literary contexts (up and down the page) and according to their genre (type of literature). In addition, however, a redemptive-movement approach discerns meaning as biblical texts are read within their ancient-world historical context—the historical side of a grammatical-historical hermeneutic. In other words, a redemptive-movement approach permits us to do a better job within the larger framework of a grammatical-historical hermeneutic.

Our closing thoughts should return to how we started this book.

The "troubled Christian soul" introduction talks about the disturbing fact that the Bible teaches the virtue of leaving marks and bruises in a good and effective beating. As much as I would like to think otherwise, the evidence strongly favors understanding adults *and children* within this virtue perspective on beatings with the rod. Most Christians struggle with this perspective and hold along with present-day two-smacks-max proponents that such beatings are abusive. This is true for adults and children. As we read the corporal punishment instructions involving the rod, the whip and the heavy knife, many aspects of them are troubling. Rather than ignoring such biblical texts, this book has attempted to face the ethical and hermeneutical issues and to lay them open before the Christian community. While there might be better ways of resolving the ethical and hermeneutical problems of these never-preached texts of Scripture, I have not yet been persuaded. A redemptive-movement hermeneutic suggests that we must *dare to read our Bibles differently*. We must read our Bibles and wrestle with contemporary application in a way that captures the underlying redemptive heartbeat, and in doing so we courageously journey toward an ultimate ethical application of Scripture.

POSTSCRIPT

An Unplanned Parenting Journey

The five chapters of *Corporal Punishment in the Bible* develop in academic terms *why* Marilyn and I change our minds about hermeneutics—reading and applying the Bible—in the process of thinking through the corporal punishment texts. Now in a more nuts-and-bolts discussion this postscript unfolds the story of *how* we changed our minds in actual practice. It outlines noncorporal methods that we and others have found effective in disciplining children.

This postscript is not a formal chapter for a number of reasons, including two especially important ones. First, while I am reasonably convinced about the redemptive-movement arguments in chapters one through five and the need for Christians to move to an alternative-discipline-only approach, I do not wish to automatically equate the contents of this postscript with an ultimate ethical application of the Bible (see Z in fig. 2.1). Yes, these alternative-discipline-only methods provide a way to discipline children without having to resort to physical hitting (two-smacks-max) and that represents good ethical development. Yet the noncorporal methods in this postscript need to be analyzed in case they might be improved upon. There is always room for growth. Second, the alternative-discipline-only methods that I will describe were developed within a highly Western-world framework. No doubt other noncorporal methods would work well and might fit better within other cultures around the world. The following discussion would benefit from a broader consideration of noncorporal methods that are effective in childrearing, but I will have to leave that for someone else to pursue. With those two observations in place I can begin the story.

OUR STUMBLING, BUMBLING, PARENTING STORY

Parenting children is deeply personal. Moments of parenting bring great pleasure and also times of incredible pain. Marilyn and I thank God that all three of our now adult children (Jon, Chrissie and Joel) have matured in their love for God and within their own worlds are living out what it means to follow Jesus. Although a generation younger, they now at times challenge our own lives to pursue God—an interesting reversal in Christian discipleship! But while they have turned out well and I am very proud of each of them, I sometimes think that this has happened more *despite* their having me as a father than *because* of me. Some days I parented well and some days . . . well, I think I did a downright lousy job. More importantly, our eventual choice of noncorporal disciplinary methods with our third child (a journey well underway even with our second child) involved not only hermeneutical and ethical considerations but also some personal experiences that pushed this ethical reasoning. I will muddle through some of these events to show how experience has affected and heightened my ethical reasoning. This personal component has not always been easy to share; some days I would rather not go there. But let me start with a look at how our backgrounds played a role in the parenting journey.

Our background. None of us read Scripture in isolation from life experience. So I probably should reveal some of the background that Marilyn and I bring to this subject. I was raised in a home with wonderful Christian parents who endeavored to do what Scripture teaches about raising children, and in the context of the 1950s and 1960s they naturally endorsed spanking. My father was a medical doctor, a scholar in the field of public health and an avid lay academic when it came to biblical studies— he has a large library of Christian books. I suppose that both his medical background and his love for biblical studies attracted him to James Dobson's materials on raising children. Thus I grew up in a family of four boys (no girls), and as you might guess, Dad and Mom took each of us boys on more than one occasion to the proverbial woodshed.

Not surprisingly, in our own home Marilyn and I continued in the tradition of spanking that was handed down to us—no pun intended—from our parents and from Scripture. During the early years of our first child we read every Dobson book on parenting available and basically adopted his method for ourselves.[1] With our second child we entered into the transitional years, during which we began rethinking what we were doing as parents. We started employing a number of (new for us) noncorporal methods that gradually diminished our use of spanking. Eventually, with our third child we completely moved away from corporal punishment, while strongly embracing alternative forms of child discipline. Our commitment to discipline was the same but our methods were now completely noncorporal.

Our respective learning and vocation journeys. So why the change of mind? In broadest terms the change developed as a result of learning journeys in both of our lives. Marilyn's journey included her background of working with children in various capacities—teaching children's church, leading a day camp for children, working with adolescents as a nurse and eventually teaching elementary school children. The final and more formal stage of working with children was augmented by her education and skills development in teaching through a bachelor of education degree from the University of Western Ontario and a master of education degree from the University of Toronto. Where we live in Ontario, Canada, corporal punishment has been banned in public education since the 1970s; today it is banned in both private and public schools throughout the country.[2] So when it came to experience, Marilyn was way ahead of me as an alternative methods practitioner within this public education venue. She developed and used good classroom management skills and functioned as a resource for other teachers. Her primary role in special education involved working with a broad range of children with special needs. At times the behavioral issues in her work setting were very challenging, and she often consulted

---

[1]For the most recent edition see James Dobson, *The New Dare to Discipline*, 2nd ed. (Carol Stream, Ill.: Tyndale House, 1992).
[2]In 1971 the Toronto school board banned the use of corporal punishment. Over the next thirty years other provinces in Canada joined the ban. As of 2004 corporal punishment has been banned in *both* public and private education throughout the whole of Canada.

specialists in shaping and implementing behavior plans. These extreme cases made our normal parenting at home through noncorporal means look comparatively easy. In short, Marilyn's practical background in education spilled over into our home and helped us both develop our parenting skills as alternative-discipline-only folk. We discovered some excellent alternative methods that actually work.

On the other hand, my theological background helped us figure out the biblical component. As a couple we had to wrestle with whether we could still be faithful to biblical instructions about raising kids (especially the spanking proverbs in Scripture) if we chose to use only noncorporal methods of discipline. Marilyn and I spent many hours sipping tea on the front porch and talking about how we as followers of Jesus should apply the Bible in raising our kids. We have together made a pilgrimage in our understanding of Scripture and what it means to fulfill its teaching and ethic in our contemporary context. As husband and wife, we have come to appreciate the redemptive spirit of Scripture and have enjoyed discussions that engage the question of what an ultimate application of that redemptive spirit ought to look like in our context and world. In short, we no longer think about hermeneutics and applying the biblical text the same way that we did twenty years ago.

A family journey: Our son Jon and dog Muffin. Then there were certain family experiences. This classroom was just as real but outside of any academic hall or vocational commitment. Sometimes God uses an informal street-smart education to help us see life differently. In this case there were two family experiences that God used to help push our thinking in this area of disciplining children. In this setting I was not the professor; I was the student! And I learned under the tutelage of my oldest son, Jon, and our dog, Muffin. God used a dog and a child to help change my mind.

Our son Jon. Along with all the hermeneutic discussions in the first five chapters of this book, an unusual experience with our son Jon played a key role in causing me to change my mind in the spanking debate. For almost the whole of our marriage I never cried in front of Marilyn. It is not that I am a hardhearted person; I just do not cry. But that all changed when something happened to our oldest son Jonathan.

It really messed me up. Unlike my past life, today I can be driving along and I may have to pull the car over because I cannot see the road in front of me. Tears, not rain, block my vision. Let me share how this change happened.

Somewhere between the ages of twelve and thirteen Jon developed a degenerative brain disease. From that point he started going downhill—physically and mentally. On a human level the prognosis was (and is) not good. Aside from the miraculous intervention of God, Jon will eventually be a quadriplegic with little or no mental capacity. While Jon's continued decline has brought what seems like unending brokenness and pain into our lives, he also blesses our home at times with paradoxical joy and profound insights into life. We see the world around us differently. Our values are different. We are acutely aware of the brokenness in our own lives.

In particular, here is why Jon's decline turned my corporal-punishment views upside down. For the longest time I held that it was legitimate to spank preschoolers and early elementary kids because they did not have the ability to reason. Thus I held what virtually all pro-spankers argue (see chap. 1), that the switch away from corporal punishment when children become older is because they are now able to reason. With reasoning abilities available, we can successfully move to noncorporal methods and leave corporal discipline behind. In other words, the lack of reasoning abilities is what requires corporal punishment methods. I bought this line of argument hook, line and sinker! Then Jon came along.

Today Jon is twenty-four years old. But due to his cognitive decline, he has functioned for many years in his reasoning capabilities much like a preschooler. He is no longer able to reason as an adult or even as a teenager. When this happened, it shot several holes in the way I had formerly used reasoning capabilities (or the lack thereof) to support my use of the two-smacks-max method. With Jon I kept asking myself why I did not simply move back to the use of corporal punishment (spanking) now that he could no longer reason as an adult. I have no doubt that spanking Jon for certain actions would get the job done. It would still result in behavior benefits. But there is no way that I could ever bring myself to spank Jon now. Even the thought is revolting to me. He is an adult, and such an action, despite his childlike mental capacity, would degrade him as a human being.

Granted, I probably feel this way in part because I have been culturally acclimatized against adults being spanked or beaten with rods and whips. Aside from this cultural inclination, however, I am also convinced ethically about the issue: the removal of the rod and whip for adults, along with a greater focus on and replacement with restorative justice is a far better approach to adult punishment. Lashes on the back do little to rebuild a broken world and undo damages. There is something extremely degrading about the thought of handing out beatings to my adult son Jon for his misbehavior simply because he can no longer reason. This realization challenged the premise for why I was inclined toward using two-smacks-max for young children but not for older children, teens and adults. If the logic flowed one way, moving from children to young adults (leaving spanking behind), why could it not flow the other way in the exceptional cases where adults like Jon become cognitive children once again (reintroducing spanking)? I was stumped.

Ironically, Jon's decline accelerated my own determination as a parent to learn effective alternative-discipline-only methods. Since as a couple we were (and still are) committed to managing Jon's behavior through noncorporal means of discipline, we have worked hard at understanding various alternative-discipline-only approaches. Of course, what we discovered in the process was that alternative-discipline-only approaches were successful with young children who (like Jon) could not reason as adults.

Our dog Muffin. God also used a couple of dogs to help me think through corporal punishment for children. I was raised in a family who at times used a rolled up newspaper to give the dog a smack if it was disobedient. So I instinctively did this newspaper-smack technique with our first dog. On the other hand, Marilyn had been raised in a family that used only noncorporal means of training and disciplining dogs. Over time Marilyn showed me various noncorporal methods of teaching obedience to dogs. I actually made the transition with our dogs a little ahead of our change in child discipline. With our first dog I slowly learned how to require good behavior without smacking her. Imagine that—an old dog like me learning new tricks from our pet dog! By the time of our second dog Muffin (a cute and affectionate Havanese) I had come a long way in my understanding of animals; I would never hit her. And Muffin was (and still is) a very obedient dog given our employment of noncorporal means of obedience training.

Okay, I have opened can of worms—the corporal punishment of animals. Sorry, I do not want to get into issues surrounding the ethical treatment of animals. (I suspect you can figure out my position and how I would get there.) This book is not intended to address that subject. Nevertheless, I do want to show how God used a dog or two, as well as our son Jon, to awaken me to my fallacious thinking about adult reasoning capabilities being required in order to move away from two-smacks-max. These dogs certainly did not have anything close to adult reasoning capacity. Yet they had their own lower-level reasoning abilities (far less than preschool children) that I could work with and train through noncorporal means. If obedience with dogs did not require hitting them, why was I still hitting my kids?

That is it—a brief version of our stumbling, bumbling, parenting story that unfolds how we changed our minds. The remainder of this postscript describes in greater detail the practice of noncorporal methods of discipline that made our journey possible. If at the end of the discussion we see things differently, let's not become uncivil toward each other. Marilyn and I have friends on either side of this question, and we need to treat each other with Christian dignity and grace, remembering that most of the long marathon has been run together (see chap. 5). We have run side by side for most of the race. Right now we are simply discussing alternative ways to configure the finish line.

AN INTRODUCTION TO NONCORPORAL METHODS

Permit me again to say a few well-deserved words about my wife, who has helped develop this postscript. Marilyn has been an incredible marriage partner for raising kids. While I went narrow and deep with Ph.D. studies in theology, she completed a B.A. in biblical studies, a

B.Sc.N./R.N. in nursing, and a B.Ed. and M.Ed. focused on teaching children with special needs. Furthermore, she has worked with children all of her life in various contexts outside our home: children's church, day camps, adolescents on an acute nursing unit and teaching special needs children within the context of a Canadian school board. In addition, Marilyn has also been my soulmate in our adventure of raising three children together.

Marilyn's experiences in teaching and nursing contexts outside the home have shown that the use of these methods is not confined to raising our particular three children. We have seen these strategies work in diverse settings and with a broad spectrum of children (normal and special needs), and even with adults like our grown son Jon who functions with childlike cognitive abilities.

Since the debate over spanking relates primarily to the ages of two to twelve, the methods outlined here will focus on disciplining children of preschool and elementary school age. Though the Bible teaches the use of corporal punishment for teenagers (and adults), I am not aware of any two-smacks-max proponents who endorse spanking teens today. So the present discussion will focus primarily on the discipline of young children. Discipline for teenagers is a crucial area of parental responsibility but beyond the intended scope of this postscript.

GETTING STARTED

If you are a parent interested in exploring noncorporal discipline, the last thing you need is a truckload of books dumped in your lap. Instead, we will pick one book (a short one!) for you to read, re-read and master. Although we have a number of introductory favorites, the one we recommend for parents getting started is by Thomas W. Phelan, *1-2-3 Magic: Effective Discipline for Children 2-12*.[3] Phelan's method is simple, effective and starts working in a short period of time.

In a nutshell, Phelan's *1-2-3 Magic* uses time-tested strategies that help parents figure out how to discipline their kids and take charge of

---

[3]Thomas W. Phelan, *1-2-3 Magic: Effective Discipline for Children 2-12*, 3rd ed. (Glen Ellyn, Ill.: ParentMagic, 2003). For further information see ParentMagic's website: <www.parentmagic .com>.

their home. I do not want to spoil your adventure in reading this material, so I will simply say go buy a copy. Read through it as a couple. Then put it into practice. It will change the way your kids behave. It will also change the way you behave.

In the rest of this postscript, Marilyn and I will summarize various noncorporal strategies that have worked for us with children ages two to twelve. These disciplinary strategies or methods fall into two categories: (1) *preventive* discipline strategies, and (2) *corrective* discipline strategies. As we look at these two groups, remember that by "discipline" we mean any parental action that shapes a child's behavior. Consequences are important, but good parenting must see consequences as only one piece of a much larger disciplinary strategy.

PREVENTIVE DISCIPLINE STRATEGIES

Preventive strategies are things that parents can do to encourage desirable behavior in their children and lessen misbehavior. Through a variety of preventive strategies parents can control more of their kids' behavior than often realized. If you work hard at the preventive end, it will pay off with wonderful returns by reducing bad behavior and thus greatly lessening the need for corrective strategies. We might say, "An ounce of preventive parenting is better than a pound of corrective cure!" I am convinced that parents sometimes bring out the worst in their kids because they have little understanding of preventive discipline. Half the battle is figuring out how to eliminate bad behavior by using proactive measures.

Routine schedules. When our kids were young, almost every evening at home involved exactly the same schedule: (1) supper, (2) devotions, (3) dishes, (4) roughhouse playtime, (5) bath, (6) snack and drink, (7) pick up toys, (8) brush teeth, (9) read a story and sing, (10) various creative hugs once in bed,[4] (11) bedtime prayers, and (12) lights out. The routine was the same every day. In the summer with more daylight we extended the roughhouse time a bit and often played outdoors. Otherwise the routine was so predictable that it could be called a family ritual.

---

[4]See a discussion of these later in this postscript. As small, insignificant and silly as we might think these creative hugs were, they functioned as a powerful force in our kids' lives.

The times were the same. The events were always in the same order. Our kids loved it. It gave them a sense of security, and it provided us with a sense of sanity.

So why start with something so mundane and boring as routine schedules? Three reasons. First, growing good habits in kids means that good behaviors must become routine. Good behavior must become a habit. Parenting with solid routines is one of the best ways to remove an easy 50 percent of bad behavior in kids. If the kids (and adults!) know exactly what is happening, when and what is next, the room for conflict over "baths and bedtimes" is almost squeezed out completely. Second, the schedule utilizes a lot of common sense about what works well with children. There are good reasons why everything within our twelve-point schedule is put where it is. Work with it a few times and you will discover those reasons. Third, this kind of scheduling connects well with some of the corrective discipline methods that we will unpack in the latter half of this postscript.

Early bedtimes for kids. One great proactive step in parenting is to guard your own sanity time. Having some time for yourself and for your spouse at the end of the day will make you a much better parent, and in turn your children will (believe it or not) be better-behaved kids. If you want to parent with one foot nailed to the floor, then go ahead and let your kids set their own bedtimes each night. Or for an even greater dose of parenting insanity let your preschool or elementary children go to bed at the same time as you. Smart parents build their own downtime into the routine, which rewards them with serenity and quiet once their kids are in bed. If possible, build a two-hour margin (yes, two hours) between the time you go to bed and your kids' bedtimes. It will pay great dividends. If they wake up early, that is fine. But they must stay in their rooms and play quietly or read until a prescribed time (7 a.m. worked well for us). Sleep for the whole household is a major step toward good behavior for both children and adults.

Calm, controlled parenting. Modeling good behavior as an adult is crucial to achieving the right kinds of behavior in children. Out-of-control parents produce ill-behaved kids. If you yell and scream while interacting with a child's unwanted behavior, you will see the same obnoxious behaviors developing in your children. Furthermore, especially on the corrective side of things, parental calm is needed in order to gain control over misbehavior. The more you control you, the more you control your kids. If as parents we fail to control ourselves, then there is little chance we will help our kids do it at their level.

Forget lengthy, logical explanations. Parents sometimes drone on with lengthy lectures to their children about how their misbehavior is harmful to themselves and to others. Your logic may be brilliant. Your rhetoric may be inspiring. But kids simply zone out, and the lectures make little behavioral difference. The temptation is to treat a child like an adult. Big mistake. Children are not mini-adults. Rational discussion does not fix kids' misbehavior the way it might help with an adult. So forget it. Learn the art of not speaking (or at least speaking less). The effective discipline of your children depends on radically limiting your words at times and then saying plenty at other times when children behave well.

So learn when to say more and when to say less. This is essential for (1) encouraging good behavior in your children, and (2) establishing control in your home with corrective tools. It is so important that I will repeat this point in both the preventive and corrective halves of this postscript.

Say more: Praise. Parents need to say more (shout it from the rooftops) when their children behave well. They need to talk it up. Our culture teaches us to praise accomplishments. Accomplishments are good, and we certainly need to affirm our children here. But a core Christian value that often runs against the grain of our culture is the ranking of good behavior (character) as far more important than good accomplishments. If our society teaches us to place our kids' good accomplishments on open display in the kitchen with fridge magnets ("Look, Sally got an A+ in spelling!"), what sort of greater celebrations and verbal praise ought we to give for good behavior? If we work hard in our parenting here, then the corrective side of the equation shrinks considerably.

You can never overdo praise for children who are acting in ways that are pleasing to their parents. So when it comes to good behavior (far more than good accomplishments!), you need to wear your coaching cap and yak it up. It must be sincere and cannot be dispensed in miserly portions. Positive affirmation must flow freely and in lavish ways like the river coming up from the throne in the new Eden that brings life to the earth. Positive strokes do amazing things to grow the right kind of behavior in children.

Say less: Correction. When kids do something wrong, that is the time to say less. I do not mean *do* less. Rather, I mean *say* less. If you cannot count your words on one hand, you have probably said too much. No lengthy reasoning about why a behavior is wrong or destructive—it simply does not work with toddlers and young children. Although there will be words, it is almost as if we speak more through nonverbal means. The more we say and try to reason with the child as we would with an adult, the less power we will have as a parent. Conversely, the less we say, the more parental power we will have. This "say less" point may be hard to learn. But it is one key to effective discipline.

Enough food and sleep. After a while Marilyn and I could easily predict when each of our children would get irritable and display unwelcome behaviors. The equation was very simple. Not enough sleep (or food) and we were destined for all kinds of bad behavior. As parents we soon learned to keep a close eye on the amount of sleep our kids got and the timing of their meals. Well-rested and well-fed kids are generally happy little people. Anything (and I mean anything!) that interferes with this preventive measure needs to be sharply scrutinized. One of the reasons we limited sleepovers for our children is that sleepovers often left them exhausted from lack of sleep. They should really be called sleep*less*overs. We soon learned to monitor how many sleepovers our kids had in a year, we required a no-more-talking deadline (when the sleepover was at our home), and we prescribed extra sleep on either side of the event in order refill their little sleep tanks. If they wanted a sleepover approved, our kids had to agree to these guidelines before we would say yes. The rule of thumb with babies, children and even teenagers: Always be checking sleep and food levels. Running on empty in either of these categories makes for bad behavior times.

Pick your battles; win the battles you pick. Please do not get the wrong impression. By introducing *battle* terminology I am not pitting parents against children, as would be the case in a war, where one side is engaged in fierce fighting against a military enemy. Our kids are not the enemy. Parenting at times *feels* like a battleground. Yet as parents we are in conflict with the bad behavior of our beloved children and not with our children themselves. This crucial distinction assists in keeping our parental cool because it helps us avoid a personal gridlock with our children.

Keeping this important qualifier in mind about the enemy, there is a twofold battle dictum that parents need to learn: "Pick your battles!" and "Win the battles you pick!" First, preventive discipline means that you must pick your battles. If you take on too many battles, you will lose your effectiveness. Also, if you take on battles that you cannot win (due to the nature of the battle), you will lose your effectiveness. When I see parents fighting with their children about eating their food, I say to myself (hopefully not out loud), *They've got to be crazy!* A much wiser approach is to say nothing. Never make food a battle zone, especially when table time in the home needs to be sacred for positive family interaction. Give children no other food or snacks between meals and eventually they will eat. Do not turn food into a battle. I could go on with a long list of "One Hundred Dumb Battles" that novice parents take on. Some of these Marilyn and I have learned about the hard way. You need to develop a no-battles list of your own in your home. Talk it over with your spouse. Read and work hard at developing this area of your preventive discipline strategy.

Why pick your battles? Well, it makes good parenting sense. Battles often take inordinate amounts of time and huge quantities of emotional energy. If you engage in worthless battles, you lose precious energy resources needed to win the more valuable battles that you pick. So choose wisely. Get help here and think long and hard about every area of conflict in your home. Ask yourself, *Is this is a battle worth fighting?*

The flipside to "pick your battles" is another equally important preventive discipline maxim, namely, "win the battles you pick." If I were in a live seminar setting, I would have us repeat these two lines until our parental brains went to mush. It is just that important. You must win your parenting battles. This is not an option. Preventive discipline always wins smartly chosen battles. The action of always winning battles is in fact good preventive discipline. I will try to explain why by asking a question: What happens when a child battles loud enough and long enough to wear you down and eventually gets his or her way? The answer is vital to learning to parent well. If the child wins a battle (any battle), you have just sown seeds for all kinds of future battles! You have rewarded misbehavior instead of good behavior and taught your child a lesson on how to manipulate you. Good parenting (1) picks wise battles, and (2) wins all battles. There is no other way to do parenting well. Such a wise move in the life of parents rightly falls under the category of preventive discipline because it greatly reduces the need for corrective discipline in your home.

Counteract boredom. Children are inquisitive creatures who naturally like to explore the world around them. Parents should be especially prepared for times when boredom is apt to set in. When parents hit these occasions unprepared, then often kids act out in unproductive ways toward their siblings or they pester their parents with that nagging question about how long will it take until we get there? To prevent boredom and its behavioral repercussions on family trips, for example, Marilyn planned ahead. The kids each got a treat bag that was at least half full of educational adventures (although we never called them such) as well as simply fun things and healthy snacks for along the way. We also had all kinds of oral road games (I Spy, Count the Animals, Word Association, Alphabet Vocab, Group Story Making, etc.) to play together as we traveled. We frequently played oral games as teams or added a nickel per animal sighting in order to increase the interest levels and bring some fun competition into the mix. Even Dad and Mom got treat bags. Inside Marilyn's treat bag was a wonderful novel or two that she would read out loud for everyone in the car. Our kids never wanted her to stop. When she did, she would stop at a crucial point in the story so that the kids were dying for her to start reading again. This was such a successful practice that even during their teen years our kids still wanted treat bags for traveling. They would jokingly ask for them using little-kid voices. By that point we got them a novel or two (and some solid Christian material) to read. As technology developed, movies and personal music were integrated into the driving routine as a limited contribution for our children. But we tried not to create techno boredom (by overkill in this area) or allow technology to rob us of the social and creative components that come from other activities. As a result, our kids were generally well-behaved as they traveled. They were great kids, and we loved to travel with them.

We had a similar approach to holidays and summer vacations at home. We countered off-road vacation boredom by scheduling entire days with activities. Each day took on recurring patterns. So our kids knew exactly what was coming and they could look forward to their favorite parts of the routine. The whole day was so clearly structured that it was as if (though we never did this) the day could have been laid out on a white board with times and events. One activity was completed before moving to the next. This way our kids got in solid reading time, since books are crucial for cognitive development. They had their own computer-skills development time (e.g., keyboarding and more challenging programs) each day during the summer. We always had two or three forts in the backyard—one that I built on the ground, a tree fort that even I went up in at times, and one or two extra makeshift forts that the kids built as add-ons. This way our kids were happy with all kinds of creative play. They never sat around the house telling us they were bored. There were simply too many fun things to do.

Technology has brought lots of new electronic adventures. Some of these are good, but again I would caution that parents must carefully structure days so that children get input from a variety of activities. We never had cable TV in our home (and still don't). Aside from avoiding the lousy content, it was our way of telling our kids that the world was full of great adventures that could never be found by watching TV or by playing games on some hand-held digital screen.

Loving relationships. I could go on with more preventive strategies, and parents in different circumstances and cultures will come up with creative ideas of their own. I end this proactive section by talking about relationships. Relationships are at the core of all good discipline, whether in its preventive or corrective expression. Children who have good relationships with their father and mother will generally want to please them because their parental blessing and approval really matter. God has wired us all that way. Even very young children vie for the love and attention of their parents. If kids do not feel like they matter to their parents, then they will start getting attention in negative ways. The drive for relationship is very strong. This core human need within children holds true all the way through teen years as well. Of course, there will be temporary assertions of children's wills against their parents, which need to be handled appropriately. But in the long run all discipline done in the context of a loving home will have a far more profound impact than in a home without love. So what you do in building relationships counts as significant preventive discipline. A strong relationship goes a long way toward preventing inappropriate attention-seeking actions by your children.

This kind of parenting takes time, energy and financial investment. So plan accordingly. Some of the best Christmas gifts were activity presents and road trips—time spent one-on-one with either Dad or Mom. I would put the activity idea or road-trip map inside an envelope (sometimes in a big box) under the tree. We would drive to see a favorite football team halfway across the United States or spend several days searching out North America's fastest roller-coaster ride or hit some of the world's great museums—once with a rock concert tacked onto the end as an incentive to do the museum thing (I wore earplugs). We would go on mission trips to far away cultures, where we would work side-by-side and together feel the pain of acute poverty. We would work together in the Special Olympics and other sporting events for the disabled. The best part is that during these times, we would talk. And we got to hear our kids. It gave us an opportunity to hear the hearts of our kids as they talked about what mattered to them and about their dreams. After those times together, it was a lot harder for them to act with unchecked misbehavior. A good relationship with kids is at the heart of preventive discipline.

CORRECTIVE DISCIPLINE STRATEGIES

Corrective discipline strategies address bad behavior once it has arisen. Some of these methods are particularly successful because they catch the undesirable behavior while it is still in the early formation or bubble stage, and has not yet fully developed. Other methods address misbehavior that has occurred in a more fully formed and outlandish expression.

Event sequencing: First this, then this. Sometimes the best way to handle childish misbehavior is simply to ignore the misbehavior and use a sequencing technique: First this, then this. There is no lengthy reasoning with the child. In fact, there is no reasoning at all. Just a simple transition statement: First _____, then _____. No more than four words. Let me illustrate by talking about our son Jon who, even now as an adult, still functions cognitively like a preschool child. When he does not want to take his medicine, we simply do event sequencing. We say four words, "First meds, then cartoons." Then we walk away and keep an eye on the situation from a distance. There is no debate. There is no prolonged discussion. Jon gets four words. He also learns that his misbehavior is not going to manipulate the situation. Guess what happens? Over time, the misbehavior becomes less and less. If the same crisp "First this, then this" sequence and words are always used, regardless of how you fill in the event blanks, they take on a power of their own. Children learn that this sort of stylized instruction ushers in a battle that they will not win no matter how long they try. Remember: choose your battles wisely, and win the battles you choose.

Event sequencing typically works great with young children. Kids soon realize that in order to move on to something they want, they must first go through what they do not want. The strategy works amazingly well within a structured routine schedule for children—our very first point under preventive discipline. Go back to the opening strategy under preventive discipline and reread the schedule. Everything is where it is for a reason. When our kids heard "First this, then this," eventually there was no fuss or fight because it was a battle we as parents were prepared to win. They knew it. As I have mentioned, the sequencing words themselves took on meaning. Misbehavior was not going to alter the schedule, and there were many parts to the evening routine that they loved and wanted to get to.[5] Children soon learn from

---

[5]We could easily have moved to a consequence for prolonged misbehavior or noncompliance. In this scheduled context, the natural consequence would relate to participating in further parts

this that their misbehavior will not be rewarded (and their good behavior will).

Swapping options (give acceptable choices). When you take something away from a child, it is helpful to give something back in its place. That is smart parenting. The "options switch" is where the child wants something that is not an acceptable choice. For example, bath time should never be an option. But the toy or color of bubble bath you choose during that activity can be an option for them to choose. When saying no to a child, parents can often sidestep conflict simply by saying something like this: "Sorry, bath time is not a choice. But you can choose either the bar soap or the squirt soap, and you can pick two toys (only two) that you would like to take into the tub."[6] We kept a special box of tub-toys next to the bathtub when the kids were young. It was part of the fun adventure of bath time for them to pick one or two items for that event in the schedule. This parental action gives kids (1) something else to think about instead of the present conflict, and (2) control over a decision that is appropriate for their age level.

No asking, plus random rewards. An incredibly powerful noncorporal method of discipline is the use of random rewards. If you do not think this works, just do a little research into why casinos draw in millions of dollars from their duped gambling clientele. It is the principle of random rewards. Of course, casinos are bad news, but why not take this behavioral insight and use it in the good context of raising children.

For example, take the grocery store, where children often act like wild animals with all kinds of misbehavior. They whine and cry for whatever they want. They take stuff off shelves that they should not touch and throw temper tantrums if they do not get their way. This sort of grocery-store nightmare does not have to be part of your family experience. Marilyn had our children as quiet and civilized as could be

---

of the evening that they truly loved. Yet a parent who does event sequencing well will hardly ever have to venture into consequences. Just say "First this, then this" and walk away. Ignore the bad behavior. By this action you are saying to the child that the matter is not up for debate. Eventually they move on, and with time you teach them good behavior and routine habits that make family living fun for everyone.

[6]Limiting the pick to two toys allows children to have a fun choice, does not leave you with a twenty-toy mess at the end of bath time, and adds a novel component to this aspect of the evening ritual.

imagined. It was a sheer pleasure to go shopping with them. The trick was simply using the noncorporal discipline method we referred to between Marilyn and myself as "no asking, plus random rewards." You tell your kids, "If you misbehave in any way or ask for anything in the grocery store, then the answer is automatically no. Even if you are good, I will not be getting you a treat every time we go to the store. You must be good kids regardless. But every once in a while if you are good, I will get you a treat." It works beautifully. Of course, this strategy could go under both preventive and corrective discipline. If our children misbehaved or asked for a treat at the grocery story, there was an immediate corrective consequence that they all knew would come. They lost the chance for a randomly delivered treat. On the other hand, this method has a built-in preventive side because the next time in the grocery store, they would try all the harder to behave well.

Collective social pressure. We are not big advocates of collective discipline, but there are moments when it is useful. With collective discipline all the kids (together) either benefit or suffer from the actions of one. This disciplinary method has a downside if the same well-behaving child always suffers, but in the scramble of life normally every child will at times bring either advantage or disadvantage to the others. Since it usually evens out among siblings over time, a little dose of collective pressure is healthy. This form of discipline played a background role in the previous story. While in the grocery story, if any *one* of our kids asked for something, then *none* of them got the (random) reward. Since the grocery store is such a temptation zone for misbehavior, we would use this added form of disciplinary action. Our children began to monitor their own behavior, and at times you could hear them whispering to each other to help one another keep quiet. Ah, kind of nice when the parent does not have to say a thing. This alternative noncorporal strategy is exactly what skilled teachers do when they require complete silence in their classrooms before moving on to the next event. If used in modest doses, collective pressure works wonderfully with no ill side effects.

Counting: "That's 1 . . . 2 . . . 3." The function of counting (1, 2, 3) can be an important part of a corrective system. It functions as a pause button of sorts. Counting permits the parent to point out a behavior that is unacceptable in its earliest stages. Counting also permits children to think about impending consequences and to become *self-corrective* in their behavior. If you have to hand out consequences for misbehavior, that is fine. But why not work with children to help them develop their own corrective patterning as they think about their actions? The counting system used in *1, 2, 3, Magic* (the book recommended earlier) will help stop such famously annoying behaviors as whining, arguing, yelling and throwing tantrums. Often a parent and child can avoid the consequence phase if an action is caught early. For example, when a child is arguing and badgering, after a definitive no a parent should never attempt reasoning. Rather, calmly turn to the child and with one raised finger say in a clear voice, "That's one." If the child continues to pester and whine in an attempt to get a yes answer, during a sufficient pause between the numbers in the count sequence for self-correction, then in the same even voice say, "That's two." Hold up two fingers for added visual effect. Provided that the nature of the misbehavior has been clearly addressed by the parent on an earlier occasion, nothing else needs to be said.

Here is where parents easily mess up. Often parents want to say more at this point rather than using the power of silence. The first time the unacceptable behavior occurs it is okay to say a few words about the wrong behavior, but keep it short. "Arguing is not acceptable. That's one [holding up one finger]." Most kids figure out pretty quickly how the system works, and within a week you will be able to stop a lot of bad behavior simply by saying the first number. Eventually you will not even have to mention the offense. Your kids will know. If you figure out how to use this disciplinary technique as a parent, it is indeed a powerful tool. It takes a little skill and practice to use it well; so start with the recommended reading at the end of this postscript.

Timeouts. Should bad behavior persist beyond the count (1, 2, 3), then comes an automatic timeout. Never threaten timeouts ahead of giving them. While we hear it in the neighborhood all the time, verbal threatening is a sign of ineffective parenting. Only two words are needed: "Take five." This example assumes that you are talking to a five-year-old child and have defined the length of the timeout accordingly as five minutes. The standard approach for an age-appropriate timeout is one minute for each year of the child's age. Before using timeouts, however, explain how they work to your children and practice them several times in advance with each child so that everyone knows exactly how it works. Pick a timeout spot that does not have a lot of stimulus (no toys, games, TV, etc.). It can be as simple as the lower half of a hall closet (take out the bottom shelves) with the door kept open and a comfortable foam or beanbag chair for the child to sit on. The child sits comfortably in a quiet spot and looks at a blank wall on the other side of the hallway. Use an egg timer with minute settings and a bell or buzzer alarm. Once the timer goes off, the child must check in with the parent for permission to leave timeout. Often the timeout on its own will correct the behavior. But depending on the weight of the offense or repeated occurrence, there may be need for additional consequences.

Some pro-spanking critics ridicule timeouts as disciplinary fluff and useless.[7] But that is to misunderstand their primary use and perhaps assumes that other consequences never follow. While timeouts are not intended to impose heavy consequences in any substantial sense, timeouts do involve real consequences. First, the child's current activity is interrupted. That interruption itself functions as a mild consequence within the timeout. Second, the timeout brings momentary social deprivation. It removes the child from any social contact with other persons (parents, friends or siblings) for a short period of time. No talking is permitted.[8] Accordingly, parents need to pick a spot where there will also be no direct eye contact with other people in order to eliminate all nonverbal social interaction for the child who might be tempted to communicate silently through facial gestures. As a third component of consequence, the timeout spot should have minimal stimuli, far less stimulus than most other places in the home. We chose not to use the kids' bedrooms for a couple of reasons. During summer activity scheduling

---

[7]For instance, Mohler calls timeouts "more counterproductive and frustrating than anything else" (Albert Mohler, "Should Spanking be Banned? Parental Authority under Assault," Cross walk.com, published June 22, 2004, <www.crosswalk.com/1269621>).

[8]Any breaking of timeout rules returns the egg timer to the beginning of the allotted time.

we used their bedrooms for a one-hour quiet reading time after lunch—a positive experience that we did not want confused with a timeout. Also their bedrooms had all kinds of fun, high-stimulus distractions. In the end we found other minimal-stimulus locations that worked much better. A fourth consequential element is that the child has to wait for the final verdict from the parent. The child must always check in with the parent after a timeout to receive the final verdict. Aside from the benefit of the cooling-down time to prepare for the verdict, the wait time allows the delayed verdict to play in the back of the mind and causes the child to ponder what is coming. There is no harm (only benefit) in letting the children sweat a little about what they have done and about the upcoming verdict and its potential further consequences. This delay adds another mild consequence to the timeout.

On the other hand, the timeout is as much for the parent as for the child. Not all parents can think fast on their feet. During this crucial pause-button time, a parent can consider the nature of the bad behavior and whether a more hefty consequence ought to be given in addition to the timeout. Furthermore, it is good for both the parent and the child to have a cooling off time due to emotional considerations. Since conflicts often raise emotions in both parents and children, an immediate dishing out of consequences has a greater inflammatory potential. Never hand out consequences when feelings are running high. Timeouts provide a mild consequence for misbehavior, and they assist in wise, thoughtful parenting should further consequences be required.

After the timeout is finished and the egg timer bell goes off, the child must check in with the parent to see (1) if they are free with no further consequences, or (2) if the severity or repetition of their offense requires a more hefty consequence to follow. Now we move on to survey a number of the more hefty consequences that can be used in addition to the timeout should they be needed.

Natural consequences. Sometimes natural consequences provide the best strong correctives. If a child touches a hot stove and burns a finger, that action carries with it a built-in consequence. There is no need for another strong consequence beyond the natural result of the action. You may still give a timeout because it is important for children to reflect on their disobedience. So you say, "You need to think about what happened. Take four [four minutes for a four-year-old]." After the egg timer goes off, you tell the child that the burn itself will count as their consequence. At such points, ask children what they have learned.

Do-it-again consequences. At times a parent can hand out a consequence by asking a child to stop and redo an action. Sometimes the best corrective is an educational remake of a scene in a film, "Okay, take it from the top please. Let's do that again." For an even shorter expression, simply call it a "Redo" or a "Retake."[9] You require the child to delete the inappropriate behavior and substitute the appropriate attitude and actions. For example, if there is yelling or inappropriate speech, you walk the child back through the behavior correctly. Everything stops until he or she gets it right. If it is disrespectful speech, you insist that children say what they want to say again but in an appropriate way: "Do a redo, please."[10] The beauty of this consequence is that it is immediate and educationally directed toward teaching good behavior through repetition and habit.

Pleasure-based consequences. The most powerful consequences will come from knowing your children well and putting that information to work. As a parent you must know what people, possessions and activities your children value the most. Ask yourself this key question: What gives my child the greatest sense of pleasure? Sit down as a couple in the quiet of an evening after the kids are in bed and make a list of the top five things or activities that each child absolutely loves doing. What do they truly hate missing out on or not having with them? Prioritize these answers in terms of weightiness and then use them judiciously. Just as computer time or the car keys are far more effective disciplinary tools than a smack with the wooden spoon for teenagers, you will find parallels for each child at any age. You just have to do some serious parental

---

[9]Morrish calls this consequence "Do-Overs," which is another good, brief way of putting it (Ronald Morrish, *Secrets of Discipline for Parents and Teachers: Twelve Keys for Raising Responsible Children* [Fonthill, Ont.: Woodstream, 1997], pp. 80-85).

[10]The following are some things to teach children in a speech redo: asking (no telling), using a respectful or pleasant tone (no attitude), articulating clearly (no mumbling), maintaining eye contact (no looking away), and so forth.

thinking in advance. Know and rank a "top five" list and use the time-out to ponder which consequence works best for the occasion.

Your child needs to realize that everything aside from basic food, clothing and shelter in their lives is a privilege. Privileges come only with acceptable behavior. For young children a pleasure-based consequence might mean missing a favorite TV show or not getting to help Mommy in the kitchen. Perhaps you let the child play outside (do not penalize yourself!), but he or she is not allowed to play in the furthest back part of the yard where cherished forts are located. Ouch! Painful? Yes, but this also gives privileges to kids with good behavior. Possibly the offender must sit out of a baseball game or a soccer game, having been benched for bad behavior. You still go and watch, but this child does not play. On the way home you assure your child of your love and that you enjoy watching him or her play. Behavior is far more important than a game, however, and sports activities are privileges. Figure out the key motivational trump cards in your child's life, and you will become an effective parent in the discipline game.

Scheduled-event consequences. A specialized subcategory of a pleasure-based consequence is missing out on a scheduled event within the day or evening routine. Earlier in these pages I walked through the after-supper routines in our home when our kids were preschool and elementary school age. One severe consequence was for the disobedient child to miss out on one of the scheduled favorites (e.g., story time). To miss a scheduled favorite, while other children participated, inflicted far more pain than a two-smacks-max swat on the behind ever could. It took only one or two of these powerful consequences to bring our children around to choosing good behavior. Our kids did not want to mess with this corrective.

Since a scheduled-events consequence functions so powerfully, let me describe this disciplinary tool in greater detail. One scenario was the creative hug time. Each night I would give my children a choice of one of three hugs creatively named after animals, vegetables or machines. Once the child had hopped into bed, it was time for choice hugs. Along with a little talking and quiet laughing (we don't want to get the child too excited) the entire hug event would take about three to five minutes.[11] I would talk to the child about his day while kneeling at his bedside and ask which of three hugs he would like. I would say something like this: "Tonight you can either have a bear hug, a giraffe hug or a bumblebee hug." They would choose which one they wanted, and then I would do something creative to replicate a hug that had some correlation to whatever their choice was. The bumblebee hug was one of their absolute favorites. I would do a buzzing noise several feet away that would get louder as the bumblebee (played by my wiggling index finger) got closer to them. The bumblebee would swoop down and tickle them just enough to have fun but not enough to get them wound up. Then I wrapped my arms around them in a warm embracing hug. It surprises me that, although my three children are in their twenties or soon will be, they each remember choice hugs like it was yesterday and still tell us how much they loved them.

So here is how a scheduled-event consequence works. If a child was moving too slowly through the brushing-teeth or pick-up-toys time, I would quietly mention that we would do the hug choices only if there was enough time and if their toys were picked up quickly enough. Most evenings I did not have to say anything. They already knew. But one little comment about choice hugs acted like a bolt of adrenaline. They finished quickly and went on to the next event. If they needed a hefty corrective consequence, I would say that they had lost their hug choices for the evening. I would not raise my voice. It was much more effective if I simply shook my head in a dejected manner and said how much I was going to miss our choice-hugs time. In the minds of our kids that crazy little scheduled event of choice hugs held magical powers because they never knew what spontaneous three options I would give them. Regardless of how they acted during the day, our kids would always get a standard hug each night once they were in bed. It was important never to remove hug time. But the three to five minutes of intimate talking and choice-of-hugs ritual was only for well-behaved kids. Be-

---

[11]Note that there is only one creative hug (from a choice of three) and then we pray together. Both the child and I would briefly pray. All this happened while the child was already in bed. Note that the prayer time was last (after creative hugs) because it was a further winding down time.

lieve me. Our kids loved those choice hugs more than they liked misbehaving.

The same type of scheduled-events consequence can also work with the reading of stories. Of course, we had a story time within our evening routine. This usually involved at least two stories. We always had a Bible story—that was standard. We rarely had to remove that privilege. After the Bible story, the kids got a choice story within the evening routine. Sometimes if a child was bad, that child individually would miss out on the choice-of-story part of the bedtime sequence, or we might invoke the collective punishment (one for all, all for one). No one got the choice story. That part of the ritual was collapsed, and they moved to the next activity.

It took only one or two of these choice-hug or choice-story consequences that were such a sacred part of each day and the behavioral problem would vanish. I will introduce one other example. Although we never had to implement a family meal social-time consequence as far as I can remember, Marilyn and I had explicitly talked about even being willing to use the supper event (its social component) as something that our kids could potentially miss out on. Do not misunderstand us here. The child would miss out on the social interaction, not the food. In other words, the child would have to eat alone in another room or later than everyone else. This is a pretty severe consequence, I grant, and fortunately we never had to do this, but we discussed the option. We even talked about how it would work with not "setting their place" at the table for that evening in order to make a strong visual statement. My point is that we were prepared to use potent measures (far beyond two-smacks-max) to achieve behavioral goals. We did not have to achieve behavioral goals through physical spankings. Choosing to discipline with alternative-discipline-only methods does not mean that you become weak-kneed, spineless parents, somehow less committed to disciplining your kids.

While I will not label it as a separate consequence category, note the social overlap with other children. Sometimes the child who misbehaves misses out (e.g., is not part of our story time) at exactly the same time other siblings are participating in one of the beloved schedule highlights. This heightens the level of the consequence and its effectiveness. Our kids rarely went for a repeat the next day.

Event pics: Event 1, 2, 3. If you want to take the scheduled-event consequence strategy up a notch, use event pics to further strengthen the impact.[12] Laminate some cards that have pictures (pics) symbolizing each of the events of the day or evening on them. This goes back to the scheduling developed earlier. These event pics are for the purpose of outlining events in the schedule. Place these pics in a highly visible location in the home. There might be seven to ten event pics in a row. This type of "visual ordering of a day" is very effective for working with children who have severe behavioral challenges (especially those with a diagnosed medical condition) or in cases where parents simply sense the need to strengthen visual structure and communication.

The pictures facilitate the event sequencing that we have talked about under preventive discipline (see pp. 148-49). They can also be used to underscore an events-sequence consequence, which was discussed in the last point. As a parent, you calmly hand out a consequence such as no story time (a hefty one indeed) by flipping that visual event card over to the blank side and clipping it up again in the sequence. The visual blank makes a huge impact. When it comes time for that event, the child has to sit out of the favorite activity or the activity simply collapses for that evening. These evening events in our home became sacred to our kids. Did this sort of consequence work? Yes, and it was far more persuasive than smacks on the butt.

Consequences that fit the crime. Sometimes a parent wants to tailor the consequences to fit the crime. This type of consequence can have an added level of corrective power because it forces the child to make the connection between the punishment (consequences) and the crime (the inappropriate behavior) at a deeper level than normal. This sort of fit-the-crime shaping of consequences is not always possible. When fashioned well by a thoughtful parent, however, it provides an added

---

[12]Both my wife Marilyn and our grown daughter, Chrissie, have used these event pics with good behavioral results in working with children with special needs. Sometimes the added visual reinforcement in the sequencing makes the communication clearer and the incentive to avoid a consequence stronger. We did not use event pics in our home because the schedule was so ingrained in our children.

measure of strength to the disciplinary equation. Let me give an example from when one of our kids started lying. It happened out of the blue. One of our children started lying about almost everything. We were shocked. Marilyn and I looked at each other in disbelief and horror. An alien had taken over the body of our dear, sweet child! Rather than using corporal punishment, we read up on how to handle lying through alternative means. Basically, the core value being undermined through lying was the value of trust. We could no longer trust our child. So we stripped away all activities that involved even one ounce of trust. Things like being with friends other than in our direct eyesight, walking home from school on their own, doing paid jobs for the neighbor, riding a bicycle other than in our driveway where we could watch, going over to a friend's house where we could not see. There were a dozen or so things. We explained to our child that all of these activities were built upon trust. Until we saw a return to truthfulness (no lying) we simply could not allow them to be in any of these situations that involved trust. As our child began to change and once again demonstrate truthfulness, each week we added back a few trust-related activities. A month or two later we had our kid back. The alien invasion was over.

Restorative consequences. If a child's inappropriate behavior results in damages, simply make the child fix the problem. If the kids push Humpty Dumpty off the wall, have them put him back together again. In the process, assess the nature of the crime, of course, to determine if it was intentional or unintentional. This distinction affects the degree of culpability, but in any case, children need to be taught from a young age about restorative justice and about taking responsibility for their actions. They must learn to undo damages they have done. Even if an item is out of their price range, kids can pay a scaled proportion from their piggy bank, allowance or work-for-pay jobs. They need to make amends in real-life terms, although perhaps in forms suited to their world. Kids as well as parents must learn to do the hard work of repairing damage they have caused in other people's lives. If you start with restorative justice when they are toddlers, they will be far more responsible in the teen years and as adults. Some of these lessons are tough on kids and time-consuming for parents, but watch the results. Teach kids that people and property are valuable. If they mistreat or damage either, there will be consequences. Sometimes the best consequences are the painful ones of restoration and rebuilding.

Kiddo think-tank consequences. One of the wonderful ways of handling corrective discipline, starting even with young kids who are in the later preschool years, is to have children work at their own consequences. Here is how it goes. The misbehaving children must sit until they come up with suitable consequences for their misbehavior. Once they have done so (and the parent has agreed), then they must go fulfill the consequences. We found this technique particularly useful when two siblings had been fighting. We would sit them at opposite ends of a long couch and have them do the disciplinary work with our intermittent supervision. Neither child could leave the sofa until the reconciliation process was complete and their proposed consequences met with parental approval. They had to do three things: (1) both children had to own up to and confess what they had personally done wrong, (2) ask forgiveness and wait for the answer, and (3) propose suitable consequences for parental approval that were agreed on by both children. In our home the street jargon for this reconciliation process was put in these terms:

- Own your own stuff.
- Ask forgiveness (and wait for an answer).
- Accept consequences.

Like an age-old family cooking recipe that never fails, this disciplinary method worked fabulously to untangle sibling fights in a constructive manner that taught our kids about how to problem solve in the midst of relational conflicts. With their bottoms glued to opposite ends of a couch (they were not going anywhere) they had plenty of incentive to work at the process. As a side effect, they learned not to sweep conflict under the carpet and ignore it. They had to work through the conflict by talking with the person face-to-face and moving toward a reconciled state. They could call for Dad or Mom only when they had completed all three parts of the process. Then we would come and listen to our kids review each part. This kind of discipline teaches children worthwhile skills that will help them succeed in adult relationships down the road. Just imagine that what you are really doing is teaching your kids a class in premarital counseling 101. Such relational skills and maturity in conflict resolution may save their marriage in later years! While it takes longer than two smacks on the butt, the payoff is for a lifetime.

Family think-tank consequences. Sometimes families struggle because they have not figured out that bad behavior in children can be related *in part* to things happening within the family as a whole and beyond the home. Parents who want to excel at corrective discipline in a constructive fashion will realize that sometimes misbehavior is part of a larger group dynamics problem. An astute parent at times blows the whistle, asks everyone to gather for a family meeting, and says, "Hold on. Something is wrong here. How can we do better as a family?"

In our home setting with our older son having a degenerative brain disease and slowly going downhill, many days were painful. It was like living with perpetual grief. Caring for one another not only meant addressing misbehavior in our children but also wrestling with how Jon's decline affected all of our behaviors as a family unit. Even with our two younger, then preteen children, we called family meetings once in a while to talk about how we were each feeling and about how we could do family better. Rather than pointing fingers, we took our motto from the *Apollo 13* movie. If you saw the movie, you will remember that the hinge point in the plot was when the crew was about to run out of oxygen. Instead of acting constructively, they began blaming each other for various failures. At one point someone interjected with a great leadership line: "Let's work the problem, not each other!"

I could have put family meetings on the preventive side of the discipline equation. Surely it fits there as well. Working at things from a family-systems angle prevents a lot of misbehavior, but let me explain how it also functions as corrective discipline. At times these meetings can be deeply emotional. They are hard work and require everyone in the family to be open about how they themselves (not others) are contributing to a problem and brainstorming about how we can fix it and become a better family. Intense vulnerability, transparency and humility are needed if anything is to be accomplished. Sometimes by God's grace the rock in the desert is cracked open and refreshing waters flow out. Hugs, tears and brokenness fill the room. Sometimes we have seen how our own behavior as parents fed into our kids' misbehavior. Sometimes we have come to understand how circumstances beyond our control have influenced behaviors. Sometimes we have uncovered things outside our home that were affecting behavior. Depending on what insights have been gained, what proactive measures have been collectively agreed on and what resolve there is for change, the consequences may be reduced either in part or in whole (at times using a special type of consequence that is more symbolic than substantive).[13] The meeting itself may be enough of a painful consequence.

Loving relationships. As with the discussion of *preventive* discipline, it is important to end this section on *corrective* discipline with a look at loving relationships. I want my kids to sense that my knowing what is going on in their lives (their greatest joys and the deepest hurts) is even more important to me than having all of the behavioral consequence stuff absolutely nailed down. We are a family, not an army. We attempt to motivate godly behavior in our children through relationships, love and mutual respect. We do not motivate solely or even primarily through authority. Yes, I want my children to be obedient and well behaved, but I do not want to accomplish obedience through military-like power. Families work through relational power as much as they do through hierarchical structure between parents and children, or more so. There is no love lost between a drill sergeant and a new recruit who is mercilessly whipped into shape. Concepts like chain of command, snapping to attention, barking instructions, steeled feelings and unflinching toughness must not to be part of any Christian family. The hallmark of a good home is love balanced with genuine respect—a tender toughness or gentle resolve, if you will. So if my daughter cried because she had the tough consequence of missing story time (a very severe consequence

---

[13]Occasionally, as an insurance policy we would suspend consequences (with a symbolic consequence perhaps) or give a probationary period as a consequence to see if within a given time frame the resolve to change actually turned into reality. Most of the time parents can read their children and determine if the repentance and resolve to change are genuine or not.

if you have ever heard Marilyn read stories), we told her we hurt too because she was not going to be there. We would be so happy when she could participate the next night. But she must chose good behavior if she wants to join us. Good behavior is not an option.

In this sort of a warm family context, loving relationships act as a powerful means of corrective discipline. If a loving parent-child relationship is the norm, then children are influenced in a corrective manner by the brokenness of relationship that happens when they are disobedient. Parents who discipline in love are different from harsh, indignant parents enmeshed in loveless power struggles. Loving relationships provide their own corrective impact. Like a strong elastic stretch cord, the yearning for a restored loving relationship places a corrective tug on the heart of every wayward child. This corrective element holds true regardless of a child's age.

EXCEPTIONAL CASES AND BEHAVIOR PLANS

Some children ought to be considered as exceptional cases. Even if the parents have good parenting skills (using either the alternative-discipline-only or the classic two-smacks-max approach), a few children will still need professional resources and the establishment of a formal behavior framework. These exceptional cases represent a very small minority of children. In such rare cases where standard alternative-discipline-only methods of preventive and corrective discipline (like those outlined here) do not achieve good behavioral goals, then our recommendation to parents is to get professional help. See a pediatrician and a psychologist for an assessment of your child.

However, let me make a couple of observations that are pertinent to a comparison of alternative-discipline-only and two-smacks-max methods. First, advising parents who have children with rare behavioral exceptions to get help from professionals is exactly what two-smacks-max advocates do as well.[14] In other words, children with extreme behavior problems sometimes cannot be dealt with by either the standard two-

---

[14]Wegner cites The Family Research Council spanking guideline 7 with approval: "If spanking does not appear to work, a parent should never increase the severity of hitting. Professional help should be sought, and/or other disciplinary techniques tried" ("Discipline," p. 732).

smacks-max methods or the standard alternative-discipline-only approaches. A more complex behavioral approach with input from professionals must be put in place. Second, it is important to note that the behavioral strategy that eventually gets implemented even in these rare or extreme cases is a *noncorporal* approach. Marilyn has helped many teachers and educational assistants implement behavior plans in these most difficult cases during her years as a special education teacher. Whether an alternative-discipline-only advocate or a two-smacks-max proponent sends these exceptional cases on for specialized help, the behavior plan that they are given to implement is a noncorporal one. In the end noncorporal methods are used to handle the most difficult behavior cases.

CONCLUSION

This postscript has walked through the *how* of our journey as Marilyn and I changed our approach in raising children. At some point it dawned on us that the two-smacks-max method was only one form for disciplinary action. While the function of discipline must remain a constant in raising children, Christian parents ought to recognize that we have freedom in the form or method. Over the years we became acquainted with a range of other disciplinary strategies that did not involve hitting the child. No, we did not have perfect children when using alternative-discipline-only methods any more than when we used the two-smacks-max approach. However, the crucial discovery for us as parents was that *we could achieve our disciplinary goal of having reasonably well-behaved children through using alternative-discipline-only methods.* We eventually came to realize that many of the alternative-discipline-only methods of preventive and corrective discipline are at least as powerful and effective, if not more so, than two-smacks-max methods.

In preparation for writing this postscript, Marilyn and I spent a summer reading and discussing well over fifty parenting books. From that collection we have included a list of about a dozen favorites. It is not that we agree with 100 percent of what these authors propose. Nevertheless, they have enough broad-based overlap with what we found to be effective in our home that we know they offer good resources for enlarging on the disciplinary methods developed in this postscript.

RECOMMENDED READING

Getting Started

Phelan, Thomas W. *1-2-3 Magic: Effective Discipline for Children 2-12.* 3rd ed. Glen Ellyn, Ill.: ParentMagic, 2003.

Further Reading

Coloroso, Barbara. *Kids Are Worth It: Giving Your Child the Gift of Inner Discipline.* 2nd ed. Toronto: Penguin, 2001.

Dinkmeyer, Don, Sr., et al. *Parenting Young Children: Systematic Training for Effective Parenting (STEP) of Children Under Six.* Coral Springs, Fla.: STEP Publishers, 1997.

Glasberg, Beth A. *Functional Behavior Assessment for People with Autism: Making Sense of Seemingly Senseless Behavior.* Bethesda, Md.: Woodbine House, 2006.

MacKenzie, Robert J. *Setting Limits with Your Strong-Willed Child. Eliminating Conflict by Establishing Clear, Firm, and Respectful Boundaries.* New York: Three Rivers Press, 2001.

Morrish, Ronald G. *Secrets of Discipline for Teachers and Parents: 12 Keys for Raising Responsible Children.* Fonthill, Ont.: Woodstream, 1997.

Nelsen, Jane, Lynn Lott, and Stephen Glenn. *Positive Discipline: 1001 Solutions to Everyday Parenting Problems.* 3rd ed. New York: Three Rivers Press, 2007.

Pantley, Elizabeth. *The No-Cry Discipline Solution. Gentle Ways to Encourage Good Behavior without Whining, Tantrums and Tears.* New York: McGraw-Hill Books, 2007.

Popkin, Michael. *Taming the Spirited Child: Strategies for Parenting Challenging Children without Breaking Their Spirits.* New York: Fireside, 2007.

Radcliffe, Sarah C. *Raise Your Kids Without Raising Your Voice. Over 50 Solutions to Everyday Parenting Challenges.* Toronto: HarperCollins, 2006.

Runkel, Hal Edward. *Screamfree Parenting: Raising Your Kids by Keeping Your Cool.* New York: Broadway Books, 2007.

Walsh, David. *No: Why Kids—Of All Ages—Need to Hear It and Ways Parents Can Say It.* New York: Free Press, 2007.

APPENDIX

A RESPONSE TO ANDREAS KÖSTENBERGER

After this book was finished, Andreas Köstenberger (along with David W. Jones) published a second edition of *God, Marriage and Family* (2010). In this updated edition Köstenberger raises three objections to my treatment of the corporal punishment texts.[1] His critique is *not* of this book but of an earlier paper that I gave at the November 2007 Evangelical Theological Society meeting, which presented in summary fashion the ideas within this book.[2] Nevertheless, his objections deserve a response. I will cite each objection first and then respond.

OBJECTION 1: STRAW MAN LOGICAL FALLACY

First, Webb committed the "straw man fallacy" by mischaracterizing the hermeneutics of his opponents. He assumed that they followed a rigid literalism by stating that if one were to advocate a biblical view of corporal punishment, one must embrace the full severity described in various legal texts. Webb seemed to think that spanking proponents operated under some sort of fundamentalist hermeneutic that required the strictest, most concrete, and woodenly literal interpretation of Scripture without regard for genre and other issues related to special herme-

---

[1]Andreas J. Köstenberger with David W. Jones, *God, Marriage and Family: Rebuilding the Biblical Foundation*, 2nd ed. (Wheaton, Ill.: Crossway, 2010), pp. 342-43.
[2]William J. Webb, "Rod, Whip and Meat Cleaver: Spanking Kids and Cutting Off a Wife's Hand," a paper presented at the annual Evangelical Theological Society meeting, November 2007, San Diego, Calif.

neutics. He also inadequately discerned the underlying principle in administering physical discipline, that is, loving correction, and insufficiently appreciated the fact that spanking is but one among many forms of parental discipline practiced.

I do *not* assume that Köstenberger has a hermeneutic of "rigid literalism." Aside from not correctly presenting what I hold,[3] Köstenberger's response misses the point of the critique. My critique of Köstenberger and other evangelical pro-spankers is that *they have not explained their hermeneutic in two key ways:* (1) How do they move from the "beatings with the rod" texts to the contemporary practice of hitting children in their two-smacks-max spanking position? Why is the *literal* hitting aspect preserved from the corporal punishment texts while other *literal* aspects are not? Why do they move away from various harsh aspects of corporal punishment instructions in the Proverbs but stay with hitting children? (2) Why do they herald the two-smacks-max position as upholding biblical authority and conversely view an alternative-discipline-only position as undermining biblical authority? In other words, I find that Köstenberger's "not rigid literalism" hermeneutic has failed to answer these two groups of questions in a convincing fashion. To label my view as a "straw man fallacy" is really to miss the point—or perhaps to avoid it.

When it comes to "not discerning the underlying principle in administering physical discipline, that is, loving correction," I respond with the following questions. If the "underlying principle" in the proverbs about beating children with the rod is "loving correction" (that is the principle), then doesn't this affirmation of "loving correction"— the text's abstracted meaning—open the door for leaving two-smacks-max behind and moving to alternative-discipline-only methods? If

---

[3]Köstenberger claims I state "that if one were to advocate a *biblical view of corporal punishment*, one must embrace the full severity described in various legal texts" (italics added). But I did not state this, nor do I present it as Köstenberger's view. Rather, what I argue is that if one were to embrace a (so-called) "biblical" view of corporal punishment *as contained within its concrete-specific instructions*, one must embrace the full severity described in various texts of the Bible (not just legal texts). There is a world of difference between these two statements. Obviously I argue that a true biblical view of the corporal punishment teaching requires contemporary Christians to carry its redemptive spirit further.

alternative-discipline-only methods offer effective means of child discipline (as chap. 5 and the postscript show), then is it not possible to
talk about ethical and redemptive development in the application of
that loving correction principle and about what the loving correction
principle might look like in our contemporary context?

Several further comments respond to the charge that I "insufficiently
appreciated the fact that spanking is but one among many forms of
parental discipline practiced." First, I admit some failure and apologize
for lack of clarity on this point in the short (30 mins.) 2007 paper. I
have never thought nor intended to imply that two-smacks-max advocates promoted corporal punishment as the only or even primary
method of disciplining children.[4] In *Corporal Punishment in the Bible*
this distinction about the precise nature of the spanking debate (two-
smacks-max versus alternative-discipline-only) has been made explicit
and painstakingly clear.

There is another side to this multiple methods coin, however. Köstenberger ought to admit the fallacious nature of this particular objection. I would implore him and other pro-spankers not to use this "we
use noncorporal methods also (and you do not sufficiently appreciate
this)" argument simply because it does not address the real issue. It is a
smoke screen or a diversion at best. Frankly, it does not really matter if
two-smacks-max proponents use or do not use noncorporal methods.
That is beside the point. Yes, nonspankers like myself should correctly
represent their view. But the appeal to their use of "multiple methods"
as *a defense of spanking* is illogical. The primary question is this: Should
Christian parents keep (or remove) spanking from their mix of disciplinary methods?

Over a lunch conversation with Paul Wegner at the ETS conference
in 2007 I expressed thanks for his *JETS* article, which does a nice job
of laying out the various methods or forms of parental discipline within
the book of Proverbs. Even though I do not agree with his conclusions
about spanking, the article is well worth reading. I will raise, however,

---

[4]In the paper (as in this book) I did say that spanking was viewed as a last resort by two-smacks-
max proponents. That should have conveyed this message. Nevertheless, this book makes this
"only one method among others" point far more explicit.

a couple points of critique within this response. First, we might want to ponder why Wegner ordered his sequence of forms of discipline as he did within the article. Some of the ordering is obvious (such as leaving "stoning" as a final option within the biblical text), but other sequencing (verbal rebuke before physical beating) seems to be more our doing today than something taught within the Proverbs. How did Wegner decide to move from "do this [form A] *first*" to "do this [form G] *last* and only if all else fails and only with two-smacks-max"? While I grant that some of the ordering is taught within Proverbs or can be logically deduced, it seems clear that his *ordering and limiting* certain forms of discipline [A to G] taught within Proverbs reflects an instinctive awareness of an incremental development in ethic more than explicit biblical instruction. Why the limitations? Why not overlap forms concurrently? Furthermore, Wegner's discomfort with and his dismissive stance toward the Bible's clear teaching about the virtue of black-mark beatings found in Proverbs 20:30 (cf. Sir 23:10) are indicative of his highly Westernized reading of the text.[5] Both Wegner and Köstenberger approach the Bible with a hermeneutic that tends to bury or hide such texts rather than integrate them into a composite "beatings with the rod" picture even if we do not like what we see.

OBJECTION 2: INADEQUATE DISTINCTION BETWEEN TORAH TEXTS AND PROVERBS

Second, Webb failed to account adequately for the genre distinctions between legal Torah texts and wisdom literature [Proverbs], treating these different types of texts on equal terms. However, while both are part of sacred Scripture, one should not interpret a legal text from Deuteronomy or Leviticus in the same way as a passage in Proverbs or Psalms. The proverbial nature of wisdom literature does not require strict literalism but rather provides universal principles about disciplining children. In contrast to certain legal stipulations, Old Testament wisdom is perennially relevant rather than something to be relegated to a now-passé stage in the development of biblical ethics.

---

[5]See Paul D. Wegner, "Discipline in the Book of Proverbs: 'To Spank or Not to Spank,'" *Journal of the Evangelical Theological Society* 48, no. 4 (2005): 726-27, esp. n. 56.

I am tempted to focus on Köstenberger's questionable statement about Old Testament legal texts being "relegated to a now-passé stage in the development of biblical ethics," but I will pass on this in my response to the matter of distinguishing between genres.[6]

I am well aware of the genre distinctions between legal Torah texts and wisdom literature, and of the impact that genre coding has on meaning. My point in looking at *various genres* within the Bible (legal texts, wisdom literature, prophecy, etc.) and *various persons* within Israel's society (law violator, fool, slaves and children) was to show how widespread the seven notions were. Most of the "seven ways" (see chap. 1) were not confined to simply one genre or to merely a one person category. Also a number of the seven ways could be (1) further corroborated by ancient Jewish wisdom literature (e.g., Wisdom of Sirach), and (2) demonstrated as a reasonable way of understanding the child-beating texts within an ancient Near Eastern framework. All of this interweave in the discussion—crossing genres and person categories— was not to obliterate genre distinctions but to keep my opponents from appealing to genre as an easy way out! Genre appeals that isolate the beating proverbs within their own interpretive genre niche simply do not work. The ideas developed in the seven-ways discussion are much too widespread, across the multiple diverse genres of Scripture.

While rightly maintaining genre distinctions between legal and proverbial material, Köstenberger fails to acknowledge the deeply embedded overlap between them—far more so in ancient Israel than in our modern-day context of law court versus home setting. In my relatively short paper that Köstenberger read, I did not develop the concept of overlapping domains. In this book, however, I have shown in chapter three (under the heading "Ancient Israel (the Bible): Forty blows maximum") that what happened visibly at the city gates with legal rulings

---

[6]The relegation of Old Testament legal texts "to a now-passé stage in the development of biblical ethics" would pain many, if not most, biblical scholars. Most view the Pentateuch's legal texts as playing an important role in biblical ethics, especially if the subject matter (such as corporal punishment) has no explicit point to discontinuity with the New Testament. Since this is such a global and encompassing issue, I must be content with commending Christopher Wright's excellent work *Old Testament Ethics for the People of God* (Downers Grove, Ill.: InterVarsity Press, 2004).

influenced what happened in the home. I am not suggesting an exact one-for-one correspondence. But the overlap was far greater in the ancient world than in our modern society. Again, in chapter four I show within the mutilation texts that legal rulings often overlap with a discussion of what was permitted within the home. We need to read these texts not from our Western framework but from the vantage point of the ANE society. Furthermore, the Western reader is brought face to face with the overlap between legal material (as a background context) and proverbial wisdom even within the book of Proverbs itself. Consider the following collection of proverbs about beating "fools," "scoffers" and "those who lack sense."

> On the lips of one who has understanding wisdom is found,
>> but a rod is for the back of one who lacks sense. (Prov 10:13)

> Strike [beat] a scoffer, and the simple will learn prudence;
>> reprove the intelligent, and they will gain knowledge. (Prov 19:25)

> Condemnation is ready for scoffers,
>> and flogging for the backs of fools. (Prov 19:29)

> A whip for the horse, a bridle for the donkey,
>> and a rod for the back of fools. (Prov 26:3)

Are we to suggest that each of these four proverbs about fools and scoffers had no referential meaning in terms of beatings at the city gates? Such a view is highly unlikely. Corporal punishment for Torah infractions was carried out in plain view of all people within Israel's society. Most beatings in the ANE—and especially those for judicial cases—were performed in public. When Proverbs speaks about the benefit of beatings for fools, it surely has a broad referent that would have included family members and household slaves, but also those who got beatings within the most public of all arenas—the place for beatings generally located close to where the elders met at the city gates.[7]

---

[7]The rod of discipline or corporal punishment was also commonly used within royal schools in teaching children proper behavior, and especially for youths who were to become courtiers and royal functionaries. Given the proximity between the royal courts (with its judicial process) and the fact that the royal schools trained youths to function within the royal palace, the opportu-

Finally, I must respond to Köstenberger's statement that "the proverbial nature of wisdom literature does not require strict literalism but
rather provides universal principles about disciplining children." If it is
true that the proverbs only provide "universal principles" about disciplining children and "[do] not require strict literalism," then why could
the universal principle about disciplining children not be simply this:
discipline children. Why must we add corporal punishment (a literal hitting) to the universal-principle equation? Why must we tie an element
of literal hitting to biblical authority and object that those who do not
do this sort of literal hitting undermine biblical authority?

OBJECTION 3: FAILURE TO DISTINGUISH BETWEEN PUNISHMENT AND DISCIPLINE

> Third, Webb tended to make sweeping generalizations regarding lan-
> guage and application of corporal punishment texts in the Old Testa-
> ment, failing to distinguish between punishment and discipline. A par-
> ent disciplines a child for the purpose of correcting wrong behavior and
> developing godly character. This is not necessarily the same thing as a
> punitive measure to be exacted for violating the law. Webb seems to be
> saying that since punishments for Torah violations (A) and disciplining
> a child (B) both refer to the use of the rod, then what is true for A is also
> true for B (the fallacy of confusing sense and referent). While Webb
> helpfully examined all the passages that refer to corporal punishment, it
> is hardly legitimate to equate passages having to do with the punish-
> ment for criminals with the disciplining of children.

How could anyone possibly equate what happens with criminals
with what happens with children? Contrary to Köstenberger's statement, I do *not* equate passages that speak of "punishment of criminals"
with "the disciplining of children." What I argue is that one ought to

---

nity for conceptual overlap between judicial and educational beatings is quite possible. We
cannot clinically separate what went on in these various social settings—home, school, city
gates, royal courts, etc. For a discussion of beatings in the royal schools, see André Lemaire,
"The Sage in School and Temple," in *The Sage in Israel and the Ancient Near East*, eds. John G.
Gammie and Leo G. Perdue (Winona Lake, Ind.: Eisenbrauns, 1990), pp. 175-76. There is
evidence for the book of Proverbs having been derived from a threefold composite setting of
home, education/school, and royal courts (see Katherine J. Dell, *The Book of Proverbs in Social
and Theological Context* [New York: Cambridge University Press, 2006], pp. 18-89).

work with a composite picture derived from all four categories: Torah violators, slaves, fools and children. None of these categories will be identical in all aspects, but they exhibit significant overlap. Chapter one demonstrates that each of the "seven ways" points can be found within two or more of these four categories and sometimes further within a fifth domain of theological usage.[8] I argue that especially where the various categories overlap, we can learn from all four categories of beatings with the rod—Torah violators, slaves, fools and children—in order to form a more complete, composite picture.

In addition, a word of caution is needed about Köstenberger's rhetoric. We must be careful that we do not import a present-day Western framework into a reading of Scripture and into our discussion about what the Bible teaches about beatings with the rod. The word *criminal* in our Western context is directly tied to criminal law in contrast to civil law (the latter being about personal suits filed between individuals in court). The Bible as well as ANE law codes merged these two categories and the elders at the gate would have handled both. Furthermore, within the Bible and the ANE world, a beating with the rod alone was reserved for civil and criminal actions on the lower end of the misdemeanor scale or placed in a compound-type punishment with other more severe measures after a beating (see chap. 3). Far worse punishments were kept for high-end criminals, if you will. So a juxtaposition of "criminals" and "children" tends to distort the biblical portrait; it does not help us understand it more clearly.

Furthermore, if we look at the language in Proverbs concerning the beating of fools and the beating of children, the same positive and negative disciplinary purposes hold true: the beating was for the purpose of avoiding further folly and gaining wisdom in life. I am *not* making a connection based on a common sharing of the singular word *rod* between passage A and passage B. See my decrying such a lexical fallacy in chapter three in a section that debunks fallacious antispanking (!)

---

[8]I could add a sixth intersecting domain of "animals" since comparisons are made within the proverbial material between human and animal beatings (Prov 26:3; cf. Num 22:21-30). See Tova L. Forti, *Animal Imagery in the Book of Proverbs*, VTSup 118 (Boston: Brill, 2008), pp. 71-75.

arguments. Rather, my argument rests on much greater overlap than the single word *rod*. It involves the overlapping concepts about avoiding folly (negative purpose) and pursuing wisdom (positive purpose) in both the adult fool beating texts and the child beating texts (see chap. 1). Now if the "fool" beatings included the referential meaning of beatings at the city gates for Torah infractions (as argued earlier), this overlapping language is indeed important as it is then *rightly* applied to Torah violators who received beatings. What this overlapping discipline language suggests in terms of our immediate dialogue is that Köstenberger's rhetorical disjunction between *punishment* for criminals [Torah violators] and *discipline* for children is a false dichotomy—now on two counts of inflated language within Köstenberger's assessment. Köstenberger advances a Western construct that polarizes *punishment* (punitive) and *discipline* (avoiding folly and learning wisdom) while in the Bible both categories were operative in adult beatings. The Bible teaches that adults—including Torah violators—need to be beaten with the rod for *disciplinary* purposes and not for punitive purposes alone.

In sum, Köstenberger's three objections are not persuasive. Instead, a careful reading of his critique raises serious questions about how his own "not rigid literalism" hermeneutic works.

BIBLIOGRAPHY

Balla, Peter. *The Child-Parent Relationship in the New Testament and Its Environment*. Peabody, Mass.: Hendrickson, 2003.

Biddle, Mark E. *Deuteronomy*. SHBC. Macon, Ga.: Smyth & Helwys, 2003.

Briant, Pierre. "Social and Legal Institutions in Achaemenid Iran [Persia]." In *Civilizations of the Ancient Near East*, 1:524-26. Edited by Jack M. Sasson. New York: Charles Scribner's, 1995.

Bruckner, James K. *Exodus*. NIBC. Peabody, Mass.: Hendrickson, 2008.

Bunge, Marcia J. *The Child in the Bible*. Grand Rapids: Eerdmans, 2008.

Burns, Joshua Ezra. "Practical Wisdom in 4QInstruction." *Dead Sea Discoveries* 11, no. 1 (2004): 12-42.

Cairns, Ian. *Word and Presence: A Commentary on the Book of Deuteronomy*. ITC. Grand Rapids: Eerdmans, 1992.

Clements, R. E. *Wisdom in Theology*. Grand Rapids: Eerdmans, 1992.

Cohen, Haim H. "Flogging." In *Encyclopedia Judaica*. Vol. 6. Jerusalem: Keter, 1972.

Copan, Paul. *Is God a Moral Monster? Making Sense of the Old Testament God*. Grand Rapids: Baker, 2011.

Cortez, Marc. "The Law on Violent Intervention: Deuteronomy 25.11-12 Revisited." *Journal for the Study of the Old Testament* 30, no. 3 (2006): 431-47.

Craigie, Peter. *The Book of Deuteronomy*. NICOT. Grand Rapids: Eerdmans, 1976.

Crenshaw, James L. *Old Testament Wisdom: An Introduction*. Rev. ed. Louisville: Westminster John Knox, 1998.

Croy, N. Clayton. "The Messianic Whippersnapper: Did Jesus Use a Whip on People in the Temple (John 2:15)?" *Journal of Biblical Literature* 128, no. 3 (2009): 555-68.

Dawkins, Richard. *The God Delusion*. Boston: Mariner, 2006.

Dell, Katherine J. *The Book of Proverbs in Social and Theological Context*. New York: Cambridge University Press, 2006.

Dobson, James. *Dare to Discipline: A Psychologist Offers Urgent Advice to Parents and Teachers*. Wheaton, Ill.: Tyndale House, 1974.

———. *The New Dare to Discipline*. 2nd ed. Carol Stream, Ill.: Tyndale House, 1992.

———. *The New Strong-Willed Child: Birth Through Adolescence*. Carol Stream, Ill.: Tyndale House, 2004.

Ellison, Christopher G. "Conservative Protestantism and the Corporal Punishment of Children." *Journal for the Scientific Study of Religion* 35, no. 1 (1996): 1-16.

Eslinger, Lyle. "The Case of an Immodest Lady Wrestler in Deuteronomy XXV 11-12." *Vestus Testamentum* 31, no. 3 (1981): 269-81.

Firmin, Michael W., and Sally L. Castle. "Early Childhood Discipline: A Review of the Literature." *Journal of Research on Christian Education* 17 (2008): 107-29.

Fletcher, Anthony. "The Protestant Idea of Marriage in Early Modern England." In *Religion, Culture and Society in Early Modern Britain*, pp. 161-81. Edited by Anthony Fletcher and Peter Roberts. Cambridge: Cambridge University Press, 1994.

Forti, Tova L. *Animal Imagery in the Book of Proverbs*. VTSup 118. Boston: Brill, 2008.

Grudem, Wayne A. *Politics According to the Bible: A Comprehensive Resource for Understanding Modern Political Issues in Light of Scripture*. Grand Rapids: Zondervan, 2010.

Hallo, William W., and K. Lawson Younger Jr., eds. *The Context of Scripture*. Volume 2: *Monumental Inscriptions from the Biblical World*. Boston: Brill, 2003.

Harrill, J. Albert. *Slaves in the New Testament: Literary, Social and Moral Dimensions*. Minneapolis: Augsburg Fortress, 2006.

Hess, Richard S., and M. Daniel Carroll R. *Family in the Bible: Exploring Customs, Culture and Context*. Grand Rapids: Baker, 2003.

Hitchens, Christopher. *God Is Not Great: How Religion Poisons Everything*. Toronto: McClelland & Stewart, 2007.

Hoffner, Harry A., Jr. *Letters from the Hittite Kingdom.* Atlanta: Society of Biblical Literature, 2009.

Kimball, Charles. *When Religion Becomes Evil.* New York: HarperCollins, 2003.

Koptak, Paul E. *Proverbs.* NIVAC. Grand Rapids: Zondervan, 2003.

Köstenberger, Andreas J., with David W. Jones. *God, Marriage and Family: Rebuilding the Biblical Foundation.* 2nd ed. Wheaton, Ill.: Crossway, 2010.

Lemaire, André. "The Sage in School and Temple." In *The Sage in Israel and the Ancient Near East*, pp. 165-81. Edited by John G. Gammie and Leo G. Perdue. Winona Lake, Ind.: Eisenbrauns, 1990.

Lichtheim, Miriam. *Ancient Egyptian Literature: A Book of Readings.* 3 vols. Berkeley: University of California Press, 1973-1980.

Longman, Tremper, III. *Proverbs.* BCOTWP. Grand Rapids: Baker, 2006.

Lorton, David. "The Treatment of Criminals in Ancient Egypt." In *The Treatment of Criminals in the Ancient Near East*, pp. 2-64. Edited by J. M. Sasson. Leiden: Brill, 1977.

Matthews, Victor H., and Don C. Benjamin. *Old Testament Parallels: Laws and Stories from the Ancient Near East.* 3rd ed. New York: Paulist, 2006.

McDowell, A. G. "Crime and Punishment." In *Encyclopedia of Ancient Egypt*, 1:318. Edited by D. B. Redford. Oxford: Oxford University Press, 2001.

Meadors, Gary T., ed. *Four Views on Moving Beyond the Bible to Theology.* Grand Rapids: Zondervan, 2009.

Merrill, Eugene H. *Deuteronomy.* NAC. Nashville: Broadman & Holman, 1994.

Mohler, Albert. "Should Spanking Be Banned? Parental Authority Under Assault." Crosswalk.com, <www.crosswalk.com/1269621>, published June 22, 2004.

Noll, Mark A. *The Civil War as a Theological Crisis.* Chapel Hill: University of North Carolina Press, 2006.

Olson, Dennis T. *Deuteronomy and the Death of Moses: A Theological Reading.* OBT. Minneapolis: Fortress, 1994.

Phillips, Anthony. *Deuteronomy.* Cambridge: Cambridge University Press, 1973.

Pilch, John J. "'Beat His Ribs While He Is Young' (Sir 30:12): A Window on the Mediterranean World." *Biblical Theology Bulletin* 23, no. 3 (1993): 101-13.

Pritchard, James B. ed. *Ancient Near Eastern Texts Relating to the Old Testament.* 3rd ed. Princeton, N.J.: Princeton University Press, 1969.

Rofé, Alexander. *Deuteronomy: Issues and Interpretation*. OTS. New York: T & T Clark, 2002.

Roth, Martha T. *Law Collections from Mesopotamia and Asia Minor*. 2nd ed. SBL Writings from the Ancient World 6. Atlanta: Scholars Press, 1997.

Saller, R. P. "Corporeal Punishment, Authority, and Obedience in the Roman Household." In *Marriage, Divorce, and Children in Ancient Rome*, pp. 151-54. Edited by B. Rawson. New York: Oxford University Press, 1991.

Saunders, Bernadette J., and Chris Goddard. *Physical Punishment in Childhood: The Rights of the Child*. Chichester, U.K.: John Wiley, 2010.

Snell, Daniel C., ed. *A Companion to the Ancient Near East*. Malden, Mass.: Blackwell, 2007.

Sparks, Kenton L. *Ancient Texts for the Study of the Hebrew Bible: A Guide to the Background Literature*. Peabody, Mass.: Hendrickson, 2005.

Spong, John Shelby. *The Sins of Scripture*. New York: HarperCollins, 2005.

Straus, Murray A. with Denise A. Donnelly. *Beating the Devil Out of Them: Corporal Punishment in American Families*. Toronto: Lexington, 1994.

Tetlow, Elisabeth Meier. *Women, Crime, and Punishment in Ancient Law and Society*. Vol. 1: *The Ancient Near East*. New York: Continuum, 2004.

Walsh, Jerome T. "'You Shall Cut Off Her . . . Palm?' A Reexamination of Deuteronomy 25:11-12." *Journal of Semitic Studies* 49 (2004): 47-58.

Waltke, Bruce K. *Book of Proverbs: Chapters 1-15*. NICOT. Grand Rapids: Eerdmans, 2004.

Walton, John H. *Ancient Near Eastern Thought and the Old Testament: Introducing the Conceptual World of the Hebrew Bible*. Grand Rapids: Baker, 2006.

Webb, William J. "A Redemptive-Movement Hermeneutic: Encouraging Dialogue Among Four Evangelical Views." *Journal of the Evangelical Theological Society* 48, no. 2 (2005): 331-49.

———. "A Redemptive-Movement Hermeneutic: The Slavery Analogy." In *Discovering Biblical Equality: Complementarity Without Hierarchy*, pp. 382-400. Edited by Gordon D. Fee, Rebecca M. Groothuis and Ronald Pierce. Downers Grove, Ill.: InterVarsity Press, 2004.

———. "A Redemptive-Movement Model." In *Four Views on Going Beyond the Bible to Theology*, pp. 215-48. Edited by Gary Meadors. Grand Rapids: Zondervan, 2009.

———. *Slaves, Women and Homosexuals: Exploring the Hermeneutics of Cultural Analysis*. Downers Grove, Ill.: InterVarsity Press, 2001.

Wegner, Paul D. "Discipline in the Book of Proverbs: 'To Spank or Not to Spank.'" *Journal of the Evangelical Theological Society* 48, no. 4 (2005): 715-32.

Wegner, Paul, Catherine Wegner and Kimberlee Herman. *Wise Parenting: Guidelines from the Book of Proverbs*. Grand Rapids: Discovery House, 2009.

Westbrook, Raymond, and Bruce Wells. *Everyday Law in Biblical Israel: An Introduction*. Louisville: Westminster John Knox, 2009.

Westbrook, Raymond, Bruce Wells and F. Rachel Magdalene, eds. *Law from the Tigris to the Tiber: The Writings of Raymond Westbrook*. 2 vols. Winona Lake, Ind.: Eisenbrauns, 2009.

Wright, Christopher. *Deuteronomy*. NIBC. Peabody, Mass.: Hendrickson, 1996.

———. *Old Testament Ethics for the People of God*. Downers Grove, Ill.: InterVarsity, 2004.

Yelyr, R. G. Van. *The Whip and Rod: An Account of Corporal Punishment Among All Nations and for All Purposes*. London: G. G. Swan, 1948.

Yoder, Christine Roy. *Proverbs*. AOTC. Nashville: Abingdon, 2009.

Author Index

Scripture Index